Authentic Assessment Strategies and Activities

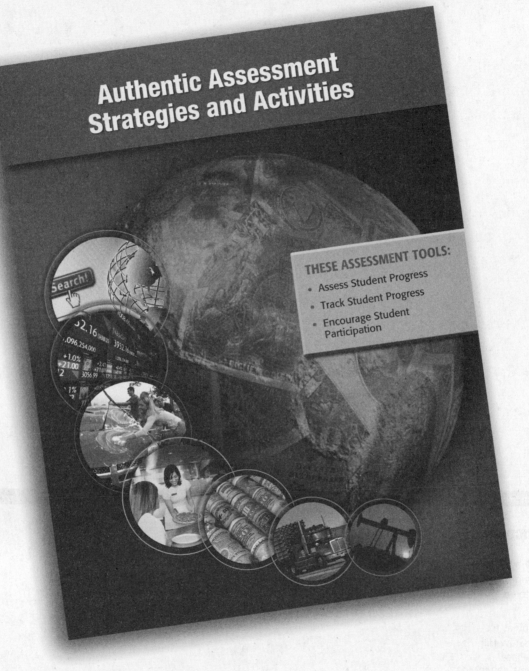

Authentic Assessment
Strategies and Activities

THESE ASSESSMENT TOOLS:
- Assess Student Progress
- Track Student Progress
- Encourage Student Participation

McGraw Hill Glencoe

ISBN: 978-0-07-895541-9
MHID: 0-07-895541-6

Printed in the United States of America.

3 4 5 6 7 8 9 10   QDB   13 12 11

CONTENTS

AUTHENTIC ASSESSMENT ACTIVITIES

RUBRICS & CLASSROOM ASSESSMENT LISTS

A Booklet or Pamphlet

A Bulletin Board

A Cartoon

A Display

A Graph

Group Work and the Individual

A Journal

An Issue Controversy

A Newspaper Article

An Oral Presentation

DEFINING AUTHENTIC ASSESSMENT

Authentic assessment is a way of teaching and learning that involves both process and product. It is not just a testing strategy.

The activities in this booklet provide a "hands-on" approach to learning economic concepts. Students will be able to actually experience these concepts rather than just reading, writing, and listening about them. Each lesson is designed to allow the teacher to give a guided practice of the concepts being taught. At the end of each lesson, the student is assigned a task that checks understanding of the lesson's concepts.

As teachers, we should not expect our students will leave our rooms quoting facts and figures. Instead, we should expect them to leave with the tools necessary to seek further information.

Authentic assessment tasks get students involved in constructing various types of products for diverse audiences. Students also are involved in developing the process that leads to the finished product.

Authentic assessment measures what you can do with what you know, not how much you know. Authentic assessment tasks are based on what is most essential in the curriculum and what is interesting to a student.

Authentic Assessment Is More Like Playing Baseball Than Just Playing Catch

Many concepts, skills, and attitudes are important if an athlete is to develop into an accomplished baseball player. A coach teaches and drills players and promotes appropriate attitudes. However, if the training stopped there, the players would never learn the game. They must *play* baseball. Similarly, teachers can present the information and skills of a discipline and quiz the students on the details, but students also must *play the game*. Students need the opportunity to put the concepts, skills, and attitudes together. Authentic assessment allows students to demonstrate how effectively they can put the pieces together in ways similar to how information is used in the larger world.

Authentic Assessment Looks at Authentic Use of Information

A common model of assessment is to teach the chapter, then stop and test the students. Authentic assessment changes this pattern. Authentic assessment is an approach to learning that changes what the teacher and students do in class. The textbook becomes a resource for learning; it becomes a means to an end rather than the end in itself.

When students leave school they will need to use books and other sources to find information on specific subjects. Perhaps they will need to make an oral presentation to a specific audience, design a display, produce a video, or research a consumer question and write a persuasive letter.

These kinds of tasks all use information in an authentic way. With authentic assessment, students are engaged in tasks in which they are crafting products. The teacher is the coach who is guiding the students' work, providing models of excellent work, and giving feedback along the way. Authentic assessment tasks get students highly involved in constructing all types of products, and this active involvement results in meaningful learning.

The word *authentic* used with authentic assessment means that the task uses information, concepts, and skills in ways that people use them in the larger world. School should be a valid preparation for what is required in the larger world.

A flow chart for information problem solving follows on page vii. All tasks require that the student follow some version of this process before the product is made or a task is completed.

INFORMATION PROBLEM SOLVING

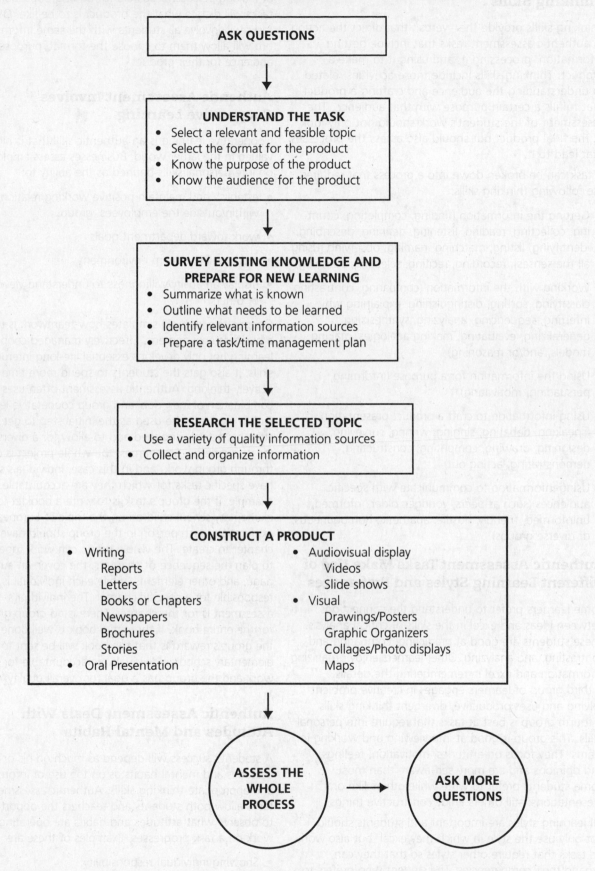

ASK QUESTIONS

↓

UNDERSTAND THE TASK
- Select a relevant and feasible topic
- Select the format for the product
- Know the purpose of the product
- Know the audience for the product

↓

SURVEY EXISTING KNOWLEDGE AND PREPARE FOR NEW LEARNING
- Summarize what is known
- Outline what needs to be learned
- Identify relevant information sources
- Prepare a task/time management plan

↓

RESEARCH THE SELECTED TOPIC
- Use a variety of quality information sources
- Collect and organize information

↓

CONSTRUCT A PRODUCT
- Writing
  - Reports
  - Letters
  - Books or Chapters
  - Newspapers
  - Brochures
  - Stories
- Oral Presentation
- Audiovisual display
  - Videos
  - Slide shows
- Visual
  - Drawings/Posters
  - Graphic Organizers
  - Collages/Photo displays
  - Maps

↓

ASSESS THE WHOLE PROCESS → **ASK MORE QUESTIONS**

Authentic Assessment Tasks Require Thinking Skills

Thinking skills provide the "verbs" that direct the action in authentic assessment tasks that include getting information, processing it, and using it to make a product. Thinking skills include those activities related to understanding the audience and crafting a product that fulfills a certain purpose with that audience. The assessment of the student's work should not only look at the final product but should also assess the processes that lead to it.

A task can be broken down into a process that requires the following thinking skills:

- Getting the information (finding, completing, counting, collecting, reading, listening, defining, describing, identifying, listing, matching, naming, observing [using all the senses], recording, reciting, selecting, scanning)

- Working with the information (comparing, contrasting, classifying, sorting, distinguishing, explaining why, inferring, sequencing, analyzing, synthesizing, generalizing, evaluating, making analogies, making models, and/or reasoning)

- Using the information for a purpose (informing, persuading, motivating)

- Using information to craft a product presentation (speaking, debating, singing, writing, surveying, designing, drawing, computing, constructing, demonstrating, acting out)

- Using information to communicate with specific audiences (such as peers, younger, older, informed, uninformed, friendly, hostile, apathetic, homogeneous, or diverse groups)

Authentic Assessment Tasks Make Use of Different Learning Styles and Preferences

Some learners prefer to understand the connections between ideas and excel in the skills of critical analysis. These students are good at predicting, comparing and contrasting, and analyzing. Other learners enjoy organizing information and excel in remembering the details. A third group of learners engages in creative problem solving and uses productive, divergent thinking skills. A fourth group is best at tasks that require interpersonal skills. This group is good at interviewing and working in teams. They focus on attitudes, motivation, feelings, and opinions and are more self-aware than most. Some students prefer to write while others like oral presentations; still others enjoy constructive things.

All learning styles are important and students should not only use the style in which they excel, but also work on tasks that require other styles so that they can expand their competencies. The student who prefers to write detailed, factual information pamphlets for peers should also be given the opportunity to become better at making persuasive posters for adult groups. Some tasks will dictate what the product is to be like. Other tasks will involve all students with the same information but will allow them to choose the format, purpose, and audience for their product.

Authentic Assessment Involves Cooperative Learning

Cooperative learning is an authentic skill that is highly valued in the larger world. Businesses assess employees on interpersonal skills defined as the ability to:

- establish and maintain positive working relationships within/outside the employees' group.

- work toward department goals.

- work well in a team environment.

- display an ability/willingness to understand viewpoint of others.

Cooperative learning simulates how teamwork is used in a business environment. Effectively managed cooperative learning not only develops essential life-long interpersonal skills, it also gets the students to spend more time actively thinking. Authentic assessment often uses a combination of individual and group cooperative learning. Group work may be used as the initial step to get students actively engaged and to allow for a diversity of ideas to emerge. Sometimes, the whole project is done through group work, and in this case, individuals should have specific tasks for which they are accountable. For example, if the group's task is to write a booklet for elementary school children on the topic of European exploration, each person in the group should have a chapter to create. The whole group can work together to plan the sequence of chapters, the cover, an author's page, and other elements, while each individual is responsible for a specific chapter. The individual's assessment is for the chapter. There is no group grade for the entire book. If the entire book is well done, then the group's reward is that the book will be sent to an elementary school. Individuals are accountable for their work and the group has a goal for overall quality.

Authentic Assessment Deals With Attitudes and Mental Habits

A student's success will depend as much on his or her attitudes and mental habits as on the use of information and appropriate thinking skills. Authentic assessment tasks allow both students and teachers the opportunity to observe what attitudes and habits are operating as work on a task progresses. Examples of these are:

- Showing individual responsibility

- Valuing teamwork

- Having initiative and being diligent
- Having integrity and behaving ethically
- Being an intellectual risk taker
- Planning actions rather than being impulsive
- Being persistent
- Showing concern for accuracy, precision, and quality of thought and action
- Demonstrating a questioning-and-problem-posing view of learning
- Showing respect for the democratic process
- Showing empathy, tolerance, and caring for others
- Demonstrating respect for diverse human endeavors, including academic arts and technical skills
- Promoting the total health of self and others
- Showing concern for the global community
- Being flexible and adaptable
- Showing self-confidence
- Valuing self-assessment as a way of improving strengths and weaknesses

THE AUTHENTIC ASSESSMENT TASK

This book contains 25 authentic assessment tasks. You are encouraged to use them, change them, and create your own versions. After some experience with tasks like these, students will be able to help create them, and, thus, increase their ownership of the process.

Following is a description of the elements that are essential for a valid task. Evaluate each task using these criteria.

1. **Essential:** The task must focus on the most important elements of the course.

2. **Integrative:** The task requires that the student put together important information, concepts, and skills.

3. **Engaging:** The task grabs the attention of the students.

4. **Activating:** As the students begin working on the task, they become more and more interested and willing to work harder and harder.

5. **Feasible:** The time, sources of information, and other resources are available to students.

6. **Safe:** The activity is safe for the student and others.

7. **Equitable:** All students have a fair chance to be successful.

8. **Balance of Group and Individual Work:** Group work is often used in authentic assessment tasks.

A good strategy is to engage and activate students. In projects in which the group works on a single product or performance, each individual must be held accountable for his or her part.

9. **Appropriate Structure:** The task has enough structure in it so students have a reasonable chance to understand it. Structure can be provided through the statement of the task, the directions, the rubric and/or the classroom assessment list of criteria (shown ahead of time to students), and the models of excellent work. These models are related to but not from the same assignment as the current task, which also are shown to the students ahead of time.

10. **Authentic Product:** The product is very similar to or the same as products found in the larger world (e.g., the product is not one that is unique to schools).

11. **Authentic Process:** The processes students use to complete the task are very similar to or the same as the processes used by people in the larger world working on a similar task.

12. **Criteria to Assess Quality:** The criteria that will be used to judge the quality of the process and the product are shared with the students at the beginning of the task. Students may be involved in setting the criteria. Rubrics and classroom assessment lists are the criteria for the tasks in this book. Rubrics are sets of descriptors that state a continuum of quality from excellent to poor. A classroom assessment list reflects the standards of each rubric. Rubrics are used by the teacher to assess a product. Classroom lists are used by the student to guide and assess the work. Individual rubrics and classroom lists to assess each type of task presented in this book can be found on pages 27 to 62.

13. **Models of Excellent Work Available:** Models of excellent work are available to students at the beginning of a task. The models should be of work similar to but not the same as the current task. A variety of excellent work can be displayed to show that excellence comes in many forms. When you first start using authentic assessment tasks, you many not have models available. Start saving excellent examples of different types of tasks so that your students can be motivated to do excellent work.

14. **Self-Assessment:** The task includes a way for the student to engage in self-assessment of the process and/or the product. See pages xi, xii and xiv for additional information on self-assessment.

15. **Outside Assessment:** If the audience for the product of this task is other than the teacher and classmates, that outside audience can provide an

assessment of the product or performance. Outside audiences should be used whenever possible.

16. **Feedback and Revision Loop:** The task allows opportunity for the student to get feedback from peers and/or the teacher while the work is in progress. This gives the student the opportunity to revise and refine the product.

17. **Connection to the Context of the Curriculum:** The task fits naturally into the curriculum and is a good way to assess a student's thinking and understanding of the concepts being studied.

Format of a Task

The first step in creating a authentic assessment task is to identify the main concepts and thinking skills you want to be the targets of the assessment. The task title may not be created until later. In a few words, state the background of the concept or topic being addressed (e.g., scarcity). Next, consider what type of product you want students to make. (A list of product options is in the section on rubrics and classroom lists.) You may decide to give students options or let them select the format for the product. When the product type has been identified, it is important to state what purpose the product is intended to have. For example, is it to inform, persuade, and/or motivate?

The next steps involve writing the procedures the students will use. First, you may want to set the scene by giving the students some background. You can see how this is done in the tasks included in this book. The directions can be very specific or very open depending on the amount of structure the students need. Both types of directions are included in the tasks in this book.

A sample form follows. The form will help you in creating authentic assessment tasks.

```
TITLE OF TASK: _____

BACKGROUND:

TYPE OF PRODUCT:

PURPOSE:

PROCEDURE:

ASSESSMENT:
```

Finally, give the students some guidelines about the assessment. Explain that they will use classroom assessment lists and that they will be given models of excellent work (see pages xiii and xiv).

Task-Related Help for Students

The teacher will keep the grades and other official information; the student should keep a log of the tasks that he or she completes.

Individual Log

If the student is given the freedom to choose the task product format, and/or purpose, he or she should keep these records so that a variety of tasks are accomplished. The student should mark the tasks that he or she chooses to save in the working folder in preparation for the final selections for the portfolio (see pages xiv and xv). The log should be an ongoing record of a student's involvement in pursuit of economic skills and literacy in economics.

The following is an example of the information that should be included in a student's log.

```
STUDENT LOG

NAME:

TASK TITLE:

TYPE OF PRODUCT:

PURPOSE OF TASK:

DATE COMPLETED:

OVERALL SELF-ASSESSMENT:
```

Individual Task Management Plan

Students may not have much experience with projects like authentic assessment tasks. The individual task management plan will provide structure to the student so that he or she approaches the task in an organized, thoughtful manner. Students are asked to state the purpose of the task in their own words. Then they list the steps to accomplish the plan. The teacher may insert checkpoints with due dates to help assure that the plan is carried out according to schedule.

The last task is for the student to identify problems or barriers to the completion of the task and consider solutions. When the plan is well done and complete, the student and teacher sign it. For some projects, parents may be asked to review the plan and sign it also. Students may not be specific enough in their action plans at first. Give them feedback about the quality of their plans and show them examples of well-done management plans.

```
┌──────────────────────────────────────────────┐
│         INDIVIDUAL TASK MANAGEMENT PLAN        │
│                                                │
│   NAME: _____  │
│                                                │
│   DUE DATE: _____  │
│                                                │
│   TASK TITLE:                                  │
│                                                │
│   TASK PRODUCT:                                │
│                                                │
│   TASK PURPOSE:                                │
│                                                │
│   LIST OF STEPS (to accomplish task well and on│
│   time):                                       │
│                                                │
│   STEP-BY-STEP DESCRIPTION:                    │
│                                                │
│   TARGET DATE:                                 │
│                                                │
│   BARRIERS TO COMPLETING THE TASK:             │
│                                                │
│   STRATEGIES TO GET AROUND THE BARRIERS:       │
│                                                │
│   SIGNED:                                      │
│                                                │
│   STUDENT _____ │
│                                                │
│   TEACHER _____ │
│                                                │
│   PARENT _____ │
└──────────────────────────────────────────────┘
```

USING AUTHENTIC ASSESSMENT TASKS

Tasks that call for a wide variety of products and performances are included in this book. They are intended to be used as they are written or adapted by the teacher. A task may be easily altered by changing the product and/or purpose. The tasks here also are intended to be models for the teacher to use to create other authentic assessment tasks.

Use a Mix of Assessment Strategies

Use quizzes, open-book exams, traditional tests, and authentic assessment tasks in a combination that will allow you to know how literate students are becoming.

Start Slowly and Go One Step at a Time

The teacher may begin by choosing one task to start with. After some experience, more tasks may be used. Another strategy is for the teacher to give the students a menu of tasks early in the course, and let the students each select one or two to do as major projects for the course. At set times in the course, each student would present his or her product or performance to the class. If the student's task called for the product or performance to be given to an audience outside of the economics class, then allow that experience to occur first. When the

student reports to his or her peers in economics class, the experience with the outside audience could be part of the report. Attention should be focused on how the tasks are helping to build economic literacy in the students.

Use Classroom Lists and Models of Excellent Work

At the beginning of a task, show students the classroom list relevant to their project. Also show them examples of excellent work similar to, but not identical to, their current project. You may not have models of excellent work available at first.

Models of excellent student work are not included here. They should come from your students. You and your colleagues could define what excellent work is in your course. For a poster task, for example, you might collect excellent posters on different topics. If two or more teachers are teaching the same course, each one can collect a set of excellent posters. When the collection is finished, review the posters and select a final set that includes a variety of topics and styles created for different audiences. This set will then serve as the models or benchmarks for excellent posters. Students in subsequent classes will learn to use both the classroom list on page 50 for posters and the examples of excellent posters to guide their work. It is not the intention that students should copy the model posters; they should be guided by them. As new posters are made, additions or substitutions can be made to the set of benchmarks. Students can help in the selection of these model posters.

Require Self-Assessment

Especially in the beginning, students will have the tendency to complete their work and turn it in to you without assessing it themselves. Require that they use the classroom list on page 54 and assess their work on each element in that list. A rubric for self-assessment is on page 53. See page xiv for more information on self-assessment.

Helping Students Become Better at Self-Assessment

If the students are not experienced in writing self-assessments, they will need training during the course so that they can write this self-assessment narrative for their portfolio. After students complete tasks, ask them to respond to the following questions so that they will gain experience with self-assessment.

1. What do you like the most about your (product)? Why?

2. What was the most difficult part about making the (product)? Why?

3. If you were to do this project again, what would you do differently? Why?

4. If you were to revise this project one more time, how would you change it and why?

5. How did you craft your project so that it would be just right for the (specific audience)?

6. Describe a situation when you got stuck and were frustrated with the project. What helped you get going again?

7. What helps you be creative?

8. What are three words that describe you as a student? Explain how those three words best describe you.

9. If a candid camera were to take pictures of you working on this project, what would it see?

10. Who was the biggest help to you on this project? How did they help you?

11. How does this project show that you understand the important concepts of economics?

12. How does this project show that you are making decisions to improve your knowledge of economic skills?

ASSESSING TASKS

Attention should be focused on how the authentic assessment tasks are helping build an understanding of economic concepts. Rubrics and classroom assessment lists can be the main criteria used to assess these tasks.

Rubrics

A rubric is a set of descriptions of the quality of a process and/or a product. The set of descriptors includes a continuum of quality from excellent to poor. There are many varieties of rubrics. The one that follows is a six-level rubric called a "Two-Decision-Rubric."

S	Superb, eloquent, unusually excellent
T	Evenly excellent
U	Mostly excellent, unevenly excellent, one or two important elements that are not excellent
V	Better than poor, one or two important elements that are better than poor
W	Evenly poor
X	Not done or very poor

Using the Rubric

To use the rubric, the assessor studies the product and makes the first of two decisions. The assessor decides if the product is more like one that is excellent (T) or more like one that is poor (W). If the first decision is that the product is more like a T, then the second and final decision is made. Is the product unusually excellent (S), is it evenly excellent (T), or is it mostly excellent (U)?

If the first decision is that the product is more like a W, then the second decision is made. Is the product evenly poor (W), mostly poor but with some better elements (V), or is it not done or very poorly done (X)? In only two decisions, the product is placed on a six-point scale.

Rubrics in this book use letters instead of numerals. For example, if numerals are used, and if a student were to make, on a scale of 1 to 4, a 2 on one presentation, and a 4 on another, someone would be tempted to report that the student made an average of 3 on his or her product. The scores of 1, 2, 3, and 4 are in continuum of quality, but the distances between each of the four levels of quality are probably the same. Rubrics are more like continuum B than continuum A, so the values should not be added together and a "mean" score calculated.

Continuum A:

Equal intervals between values:

1	2	3	4

Continuum B:

Unequal intervals between values

1	2		3	4		5	6

Consider the ratings made by this student on seven posters done throughout the course:

W   U   T   U   U   T   T

It would be correct to describe the student's long-term performance by reporting that he or she made three **Ts,** three **Us,** and a **W.** Another observation would be that the rating of **T** was earned during the later part of the course, which showed that the student improved with time and practice.

A rubric is designed to lay out a continuum of quality from very excellent to very poor. It is a tool that puts this continuum into words and a tool that can be used to place students' work on a continuum of quality. If two or more teachers are assessing the same type of performance such as a poster, then using the same rubric for the posters will help them both view posters in the same way. Once a rubric has been created, it can be used unaltered by many teachers. (Even teachers at different grade levels and/or teaching different subjects can use the same rubric such as the sample one for a poster. Use of a common rubric can provide continuity of teaching and learning from grade to grade and from subject to subject.)

The following rubric for a poster is used here as an example.

S: The poster is outstanding, creative, and communicates information to the audience in an eloquent manner.

T: The theme of the poster is clear when you first look at it. As you study it, more and more information comes out. There are main ideas (the general) supported by appropriate details (the specific). There is a "wholeness" about the poster, and it is not just a collection of pieces. Main ideas are connected to a theme. Information is complete and accurate. The concepts and information used show that the student clearly understands the core curriculum related to this project. Space, shapes, textures, and colors are used to provide information and to make the poster easier for the viewer to understand. Pictures, photographs, drawings, diagrams, graphs, and other devices add clarity and information. The words used are appropriate for the topic and audience. The form of the poster is appropriate for the author's intended purpose. The work is very neat and presentable.

U: The poster is as good as a poster receiving a rating of T, but there are one or two important elements that are not as well developed.

V: The poster is similar to a poster receiving a rating of W, but there are some important elements that are more well developed.

W: The poster is difficult to understand even when its purpose is explained by the author. The poster seems like a collection of pieces without clear main ideas hooking them together. Some information may be incomplete or inaccurate. The student does not demonstrate a mastery of the core curriculum related to this project. Space, shapes, textures, and colors are not used or used in an appropriate manner to add information to the poster or make it easier for the audience to understand. Pictures, photographs, drawings, diagrams, graphs, and other devices are not used or used inappropriately. The words used are not clear. The form of the poster may not be the best one for the author's intended purpose. The work is not neat and presentable.

X: The poster is not done or is very poorly done.

Classroom Assessment Lists

The rubric is not a tool for students. Each teacher who uses the rubric makes his or her own classroom assessment list. That classroom assessment list uses terms the students can easily understand. Classroom lists are guidelines. If a student meets every guideline of a classroom list in an excellent manner, the product would probably be assessed as a **T**.

While the rubric remains unchanged from teacher to teacher, the classroom assessment lists will likely differ from teacher to teacher. The teacher decides how best to translate the rubric into a useful list of guidelines for a particular class of students. It should be noted that after a few experiences using classroom assessment lists, the students working either alone or in cooperative groups can make their own lists of guidelines, thus, further engaging them in active learning. A sample classroom lists that was developed from the sample rubric for a poster follows.

SAMPLE CLASSROOM ASSESSMENT LIST FOR A POSTER

1. The main theme is clear when you first look at it.

2. Appropriate and accurate main ideas support the theme.

3. There is a wholeness about the poster. It does not seem like a disorganized collection of information.

4. The information in the poster is accurate and shows that the student thoroughly understands the concepts.

5. Space, shapes, textures, and colors provide information themselves and add to the overall effectiveness of the poster.

6. Pictures, photographs, drawings, diagrams, graphs, or other similar devices add to the overall effectiveness of the poster.

7. The format of the poster is appropriate to the task and to the audience for which it is intended.

8. The poster is very neat and presentable

9. The poster is creative and interesting.

Classroom assessment lists included in this book allow space for you to give possible and earned points for each item on the list.

Student's Self-Assessment

An important life skill is the ability to self-assess and plan for improvement. Students often complete their assignments expecting the teacher to grade and return them. Students should learn to thoughtfully study their own work and identify what they have done well and where they need improvement. When students are taught to use the instructions in the authentic assessment task, the classroom assessment list, and the models of excellence to assess their own projects, their self-assessment will be more effective.

One successful strategy for teaching students how to use these tools is to show them posters from a previous year or another class that were rated as **V** or **U**. Without telling the class what ratings the posters were given, organize the students into small cooperative groups to assess the posters, using the classroom assessment lists and models of excellent posters. Involve the class in a discussion of the strengths and weaknesses of each sample poster. Then, when students make their own posters, use cooperative groups for peer-assessment. Require that the student assess his or her own work on each element of the classroom assessment list before it is submitted to the teacher. This process can be used with any other type of product.

Rubrics and classroom assessment lists for self-assessment are included on pages 53 to 54. Use the classroom list and collect samples of perceptive, thoughtful self-assessments to use as models of what well-done self-assessments are like.

Self-Assessment of Attitudes and Mental Habits

Refer to the list of attitudes and mental habits on pages viii and ix. Select the ones you want to emphasize and include them in the introduction to the economics course. Periodically throughout the course, ask the students to consider the quality of one of their attitudes or mental habits. At times the teacher selects the attitude or mental habit to assess. Students make the selection other times.

Attitudes and mental habits cannot be observed directly, but only inferred through observing a student's behavior and the quality of his or her product or performance. Students know best what is "in their heads and hearts." Ask them to assess the attitudes and mental habits that they are concentrating on when they work on given tasks. The following sample self-rating form has three levels of performance: **Very Well, Satisfactory,** and **Not Yet.** After the student has rated himself or herself on an attitude or mental habit, he or she then writes an action plan for personal improvement that includes a description of how he or she will know if that improvement has taken place. Do not grade these self-assessments. Encourage students to be honest and perceptive.

SELF-ASSESSMENT OF ATTITUDES AND MENTAL HABITS

NAME: _____

ATTITUDE OR MENTAL HABIT BEING ASSESSED:

HOW DO I ASSESS THIS ATTITUDE OR MENTAL HABIT?

OVERALL, HOW AM I DOING?

VERY WELL _____

SATISFACTORY _____

NOT YET _____

HERE IS MY ACTION PLAN TO IMPROVE:

SIGNED:

THE PORTFOLIO

Portfolios are a good way to look at the overall work of a student. Care must be taken to not just collect items in a folder and call it a portfolio. There must be a plan for how the portfolio will be used. One strategy is to have each student save a variety of his or her best work in a "working folder" during the course. Each of these pieces will have already gone through the assessment and grading process. Near the end of the course, the teacher asks the student to select a small number of products that best show how competent he or she has become in using concepts and information from the economics course and how thoughtful he or she has been in making decisions that contribute to his or her total understanding and the understanding of others.

When the student has made the selection, that student writes a narrative explaining why those items were chosen and how they demonstrate the degree to which an understanding of economic concepts has been achieved. The teacher reads the student's narrative and writes a short response to the student about how honest and perceptive the student has been. The portfolio and student's narrative could be used for a significant part of the final grade for the course. This portfolio strategy engages the student in decision making, promotes self-analysis, and requires a reasonable amount of work from the teacher.

If you plan to use the portfolio strategy, explain this assignment near the beginning of the course. Show the students the rubric and classroom assessment list for self-assessment (see pages 53 and 54). Focus on the idea that the portfolio will be a small collection of a variety of items that will demonstrate how the student understands economic concepts.

Difficult-to-Store Products in the Portfolio

Some items such as written reports, journals, and booklets will fit easily into a portfolio folder. Other items such as posters and displays may be physically too large to place in the folder. Oral presentations may not have been saved on tape. If possible, students should keep photographs of their very best works that do not fit into the portfolio. If this is not possible, then the student can only refer to those products and/or performances on the cover of the portfolio and in the self-assessment narrative. Another strategy is for students to scan their papers onto a CD-ROM disc and use an appropriate video camera to place still or action visuals with or without sound on the CD-ROM disc. This technology will expand the potential for what could be kept in a portfolio.

Portfolio Cover

The purpose of the portfolio is for the student to show the degree to which he or she understands economic concepts. Near the end of the course, the student selects six to eight items from the working folder to place into the portfolio. The student also writes a cover form that lists the contents of the portfolio and provides an explanation of how the items in the portfolio show how much he or she understands about economic concepts.

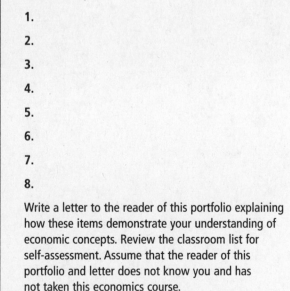

COVER PAGE FOR THE ECONOMICS PORTFOLIO

NAME: DATE:

CONTENTS OF THIS PORTFOLIO:

ITEM DESCRIPTION:

Note: If some items do not fit into the portfolio, provide photographs or descriptions of your work. Show your best work to prove your understanding of economic concepts.

1.

2.

3.

4.

5.

6.

7.

8.

Write a letter to the reader of this portfolio explaining how these items demonstrate your understanding of economic concepts. Review the classroom list for self-assessment. Assume that the reader of this portfolio and letter does not know you and has not taken this economics course.

GRADES

A teacher may also need to give a grade for the project. On each classroom assessment list there is opportunity for the teacher to assign a point value to each element on the list. Students are awarded points according to the quality of their work relevant to that element. The teacher can assign more or fewer points to an element on the list, thereby weighing its value in the total score.

Points earned by a student should reflect the letter assessment from the rubric.

The authentic assessment system, composed of the statement of the task, the rubric, the classroom assessment list, and the models of excellence, is intended to give students clear guidelines on how to engage in and complete an assignment. Feedback according to these elements given through self-assessment, peer-assessment, assessment from the teacher, and/or assessment from the target audience is important and useful information for a student to receive.

USING THIS BOOK

Starting on page 1, authentic assessment tasks are suggested. In all, there are 25 activities. On pages 27 to 62, rubrics and classroom lists are provided for use with each performance task.

AUTHENTIC ASSESSMENT — ACTIVITY 1

SCARCITY

▼ BACKGROUND

We cannot have everything we want because society does not have the resources to produce everything people want. The problem of dealing with scarcity involves making choices.

▼ MATERIALS

Play-Doh, colored construction paper, white typing paper, ink pens, marking pens, drinking straws, and stick pins; any table or space large enough to hold the products that students will produce

▼ OBJECTIVES

After completing this activity, students will be able to

- Demonstrate understanding of the basic economic questions facing every nation's economic system.
- Apply the factors of production to a given production process.
- Demonstrate understanding of want (demand) versus needs (scarcity).
- Discriminate among the various economic models of traditional, command, and mixed market economies.

PROCEDURE

1. Organize the class into groups of three and hand out Play-Doh in varying amounts to each group.

2. Give students the following directions:

   "You are to create an original product."

   "Do not create products that will not sell."

   "Your products will be shown to the class."

   "You will put a name and price on your product that you will share with the class."

   "You will fill out a form given to you."

   Watch students make products. Praise some. Tell others to work harder (even if they are working).

3. Hand out a form that asks their name, name of product, name of company they are working for, price of product, what tools they used to make the product, and how long it took them to make the product.

4. Debrief the class:

   What is Play-Doh? (a resource)

   Did some get more Play-Doh than others?

   Did you share (trade) the Play-Doh you had available?

   Did you ask others to share (trade) their Play-Doh with you?

   Use these questions as the basis for a discussion focusing on the scarcity of resources. There are simply not enough resources to go around.

5. Have students go to the front of the room to show their products, and give the name of the product and the price. When they are finished demonstrating their product, have them hold their product up for inspection, then place the product on the display area and sit down.

6. Conclude the activity by asking: What has this activity taught you about the availability of resources?

◉ Assessment

1. Students will create an original product and plan for its distribution.

2. Students will use a classroom self-assessment list to evaluate the invention.

AUTHENTIC ASSESSMENT — ACTIVITY 2

THE GOALS OF THE ECONOMY

▼ BACKGROUND

The success of any economic system depends on its ability to satisfy the needs of its people. These needs are in part defined by the goals a society sets for itself.

▼ MATERIALS

A copy of the Preamble to the Constitution; approximately 10 articles that illustrate the government's attempt to accomplish the goals of the economy

▼ OBJECTIVES

After completing this activity, students will be able to

- Distinguish between a goal and a characteristic.
- Describe the goals of our free enterprise system.
- List the major characteristics of our free enterprise system.

PROCEDURE

1. Brainstorm laws that REGULATE business and consumers. Write these on the chalkboard. Discuss with the class what they all have in common. (protection)

2. Brainstorm things that the various levels of government PROVIDE. Write these on the chalkboard. Discuss with the class what these things have in common. (protection and well-being)

3. Distribute copies of the Preamble to the Constitution and explain each segment of the Preamble:

   We, the People, of the United States, in Order to form a more perfect Union (in order to be a better country), establish Justice (make laws fair and equal), insure domestic Tranquillity (peace at home) provide for the common defense (provide protection, a military), promote the general Welfare (make sure people have basic things like health care, food, shelter), and secure the blessings of Liberty to ourselves and our Posterity (make sure people have basic freedoms, not only now but in the future as well) do ordain and establish this Constitution for the United States of America.

   Take each of the segments, and let the students decide what each segment means. Then say: These were GOALS the Founders had for our government. They only hoped our government could provide and protect its people.

4. Write the goals on the board: efficiency, growth, security, equity, stability, and individual freedom. Have your students describe in personal terms what these words mean to them. Their descriptions should be of a personal nature, not economic. They are to simply look at these terms and define them in personal terms. Have some of the students share their definitions and then relate them to the goals of the economy. Be sure to explain that not all goals are achieved, that is why they are called goals.

5. Go on to discuss the CHARACTERISTICS of our system: choice, private property, profit, and competition.

6. Let the students pick one or two partners. The 10 articles that you have gathered should be stationed around the room. The students should make their way around the room, reading the articles and determining what goal is being attempted. There will probably be more than one goal in each article, so have the students justify why they choose the goal(s) that they did. If working in pairs, have one student read the article and the other write the answers.

◉ Assessment

1. Have the partners give their answers and justifications. Make sure that the one who reads does the presenting.

AUTHENTIC ASSESSMENT ACTIVITY 3

BUSINESS ORGANIZATIONS

▼ BACKGROUND

American business organizations can take any of three major forms: sole proprietorships, partnerships, or corporations.

▼ MATERIALS

A chart showing the definitions, characteristics, advantages, and disadvantages of the three types of business organizations, with the pieces cut up and placed in envelopes; a list of 30 local or national businesses, most of which will be sole proprietorships

▼ OBJECTIVES

After completing this activity, students will be able to

- Compare the advantages and disadvantages of the three types of businesses.
- Explain the responsibilities of launching an entrepreneurship.

PROCEDURE

1. Discuss with the students what it is like to do a project alone (advantages and disadvantages).

2. Ask if any of them have ever done a major project with a partner. Again discuss the advantages and disadvantages. Finally, generate a discussion about doing group projects, once again talking about the advantages and disadvantages.

3. Organize the class into groups. Give each group a copy of the chart with the pieces inside. Let them try to piece it together. They should find the names of the business organizations, a definition for each, characteristics of each, and advantages and disadvantages of each. This activity allows the students time to discuss what they as a group would consider an advantage or a disadvantage. Give the groups about 15 minutes to complete the chart; give a surprise to the group who comes the closest to being correct.

4. Put the correct chart on the chalkboard, and explain it as they copy it.

5. Next, distribute the list of businesses that you have prepared. Have the students decide if the businesses listed are sole proprietorships, corporations, or partnerships. Ask: Why do most of us assume that there are more corporations than any other form? Perhaps this would lead you into a discussion of the Fortune 500 or into franchises.

◉ Assessment

1. Have students check with local businesses to determine whether they are sole proprietorships, partnerships, or corporations.

2. Have students survey members of the business community to find their perceptions about the advantages and disadvantages of their particular business organization.

AUTHENTIC ASSESSMENT | ACTIVITY 4

GRAPHING THE LAW OF DEMAND

▼ BACKGROUND

Graphs help us visualize information quickly. They also present material in an alternative manner that helps us understand what we are reading.

▼ OBJECTIVES

After completing this activity, students will be able to
- Graph a demand curve.
- Illustrate shifts in a demand curve.

▼ MATERIALS

Black, blue, red, and lavender yarn; 40 to 50 pennies; white string; tape (optional)

PROCEDURE

1. Before class, arrange the chairs around the classroom in a circle, leaving the center of the room open for work. Student teams will use the classroom floor as an area to create supply and demand graphs.

2. Organize the class into teams of four or five students. Assign the following roles to each of the team members.

   a. floor leader   **b.** spokesperson   **c.** observer/recorder   **d.** team adviser(s)

3. Give each floor leader two yards of black yarn, one yard of each of the other colored yarns, 10 pennies, a small ball of white string, and tape. The materials should be used for the following:

   - Black yarn—X and Y axes of a graph grid
   - Red yarn—demand shift (Red shifts right)
   - Pennies—show price/quantity points
   - Blue yarn—demand curve
   - Lavender yarn—demand shift (Lavender shifts left)
   - String—marks graph grid

4. Instruct the floor leaders and spokespersons to take their issued materials to the center floor area directly in front of where their teammates are sitting. The team will then proceed as follows:

   a. Floor leader and spokesperson will use issued materials to construct a graph grid with the black yarn and the string on the floor in front of their teammates. Tape may be used to secure the yarn to the floor.

   b. Spokesperson will then sit with the other team members, leaving the floor leader to perform all other physical tasks with verbal assistance and advice from seated teammates.

   c. Observers will remain seated and record all the conversation heard from teammates.

5. Distribute copies of the following scenarios to be graphed to each group:

   a. At $27, consumers demand 10 compact discs.
   b. At $24, consumers demand 13 discs.
   c. At $21, consumers demand 18 discs.
   d. At $15, consumers demand 37 discs.
   e. At $6, consumers demand 162 discs.
   f. At $3, consumers demand 300 discs.
   g. Assume that everyone receives a 10 percent income tax refund from the government.
   h. Assume that a new invention is put on the market that has better sound quality than compact discs.

6. Instruct the teams to construct a demand curve properly on the chart using the string and the pennies.

◉ Assessment

1. Each group will select a product, make a simple demand schedule, create a graph of the demand curve, and orally present their scenario including:

   a. a demand curve
   b. a shift right (with an explanation)
   c. a shift left (with an explanation)

AUTHENTIC ASSESSMENT · ACTIVITY 5

SUPPLY

▼ BACKGROUND

Economists want to know how much of a certain product sellers are willing to supply at each and every price.

▼ MATERIALS

12 sheets of newspaper, 12 feather-shaped pieces of yellow paper, 12 feather-shaped pieces of red paper, 12 feather-shaped pieces of blue paper, tape, play money ($15 in quarters, dimes, and nickels; $30 in $1 bills)

▼ OBJECTIVES

After completing this activity, students will be able to

• Understand the concept of supply.
• Describe the factors that affect supply.
• Develop a supply curve.

PROCEDURE

1. Organize the class into two groups. Half will be sellers and half will be buyers.

2. Set all the items on a desk and price them as follows: a sheet of newspaper for $.05, a piece of tape for $.05, a yellow feather for $.50, a red feather for $1.50, and a blue feather for $2. Explain that each yellow feather is worth one extra credit point, each red is worth three extra credit points, and each blue is worth four extra credit points.

3. Distribute $15 in varying amounts to the sellers. Tell sellers that they are producers of hats. (Show them how to fold a newspaper hat and to decorate it with one or more feathers.)

4. Explain that the maximum they can charge for a hat is $3. Have them buy the items they need, make the hats, label each with a price, and display them at the front of the room.

5. Distribute $15 to the buyers. Have them buy the hats and give the money to the sellers.

6. Raise the price of yellow feathers to $1 apiece. Then tell the sellers that they can charge any price they choose for their product.

7. The sellers who have money may buy the materials, make hats, price them, and display them at the front of the room. If two or more sellers decide to pool their resources, let them.

8. Distribute the rest of the dollar bills to the buyers. Have them buy whatever they can. Again, if two or more buyers pool their resources, let them.

9. Tell sellers to pay back the teacher's initial investment and to buy extra-credit feathers with their profits.

10. Discuss the simulation by asking the students about the economic concepts they observed. If students fail to mention any of the following concepts—supply and demand, production costs, cost-push inflation, price passed on to the consumer, formation of partnerships, scarcity, price ceilings, and consumer needs—point them out.

◉ Assessment

1. With the class, produce a supply curve based on the simulation.

2. Have students choose a product, such as crude oil or microchips, and research shifts in its supply. Then direct them to do a supply curve on a poster and explain why shifts occurred.

AUTHENTIC ASSESSMENT — ACTIVITY 6

CONSUMER RIGHTS AND RESPONSIBILITIES

RUBRICS
writing (list, letter, etc.), oral presentation, research, group work

▼ BACKGROUND

Now that caveat emptor (let the buyer beware) is no longer the motto of the marketplace, and an increased interest in consumer protection has taken the form of more government regulation, producers have greater responsibility for their products. Written warranties are offered on many items. It is, therefore, useful to know how to read and understand these warranties so that consumers can protect themselves if a product is defective.

▼ MATERIALS

Copies of warranties for different types of merchandise and services; pictures of products

▼ OBJECTIVES

After completing this activity, students will be able to

- Define and differentiate among full, limited, implied, and extended warranties.
- Alert consumers (the students) to their responsibilities concerning warranties.

PROCEDURE

1. Discuss the following with the class: What is a warranty? (*Many students may volunteer that a warranty is a guarantee.*) What products are likely to have warranties? (*Students might suggest small appliances, a car, a computer, luggage, etc.*) Why should one compare warranties? Does the warranty raise the price? What exactly does the warranty cover? If repairs are included in the warranty, does the consumer need to ship the product to the place of repair and, if so, who is to pay shipping costs?

2. Organize the students into small groups and give each group a warranty. Students should read, locate, and explain the following: What is covered by the particular warranty? How long does the warranty last? What kind of warranty is it? (full, limited, extended, etc.) Are there any restrictions, limitations, or exceptions? Does your state have any special laws that give additional rights? Is product registration necessary? Are there words in the warranty that you do not understand?

3. Reassemble the class. Distribute pictures of products or have students select pictures from a hat. Have each student write a warranty for his or her product and exchange it with another student for evaluation. Evaluating students will then try to understand the warranty and explain to the class in an oral presentation what the "seller" is offering.

4. Organize the class into groups of three to five students each. Give each group the name of a product and the following instructions: One individual in each group will be the consumer asking questions about price and warranty while the others will play the role of clerks in various stores. Clerks will play their roles as follows:

   a. Specialty store clerk will be very knowledgeable of product.
   b. Upscale store clerk will be somewhat knowledgeable of product.
   c. Discount store clerk is also a "stocker"; has no special knowledge.
   d. Warehouse clerk has little or no knowledge. Customers review material on their own.

5. As an enrichment activity, you may wish to have students research their state's consumer protection laws and present their findings to the class.

◉ Assessment

1. Have students write a list of the problems encountered with warranties based on their class exercises. Ask them to write a response to the following: How does a good consumer show responsibility in resolving these problems?

2. Have students write a letter of inquiry or a letter of complaint about a product.

AUTHENTIC ASSESSMENT | ACTIVITY 7

THE PRODUCTION PROCESS

▼ BACKGROUND

Moving goods from where they are produced to the consumer who buys them involves channels of distribution. These channels involve several intricate steps.

▼ MATERIALS

List of consumer goods; scissors, poster board, glue, magazines, newspapers, and catalogs

▼ OBJECTIVES

After completing this activity, students will be able to

- Trace the production process from raw materials to the consumer.
- Identify the stages of the production process and explain the difference between wholesale and retail distribution.
- Illustrate channels of distribution with respect to producers, wholesalers, and retailers including the following:
  a. storage and transportation processing (warehousing)
  b. club warehousing
  c. direct marketing (catalogs)
- Decide "place to sell" and "alternative" selling place.

PROCEDURE

1. Brainstorm with the class various products students might purchase in the marketplace. (*food, furniture, clothing, jewelry, etc.*)

2. Choose one of the products the students have mentioned and model it on the chalkboard. For example, draw a hamburger using colored chalk. Then explain each ingredient used and how the ingredient travels through the production process from raw goods producer (e.g., lettuce), through warehousing, to the consumer.

3. Organize the class into teams or groups of five or less, and from the list generated during the brainstorming process, have each group choose a product to trace through the production and distribution process. Each group member will select a role in producing the product. Possible roles include: raw goods producer, a manufacturer, storage and transportation middle persons, a retailer, etc.

4. Instruct the teams to illustrate the stages of the production process for their product on poster board. Teams will need to make a group decision on the "best" place to sell their product.

5. As an enrichment activity, you may wish to have students present the production for a particular product, using a slide show or a photo essay.

◉ Assessment

1. Have each team select a spokesperson. This individual will come to the front of the room and present the group's product, using the production process poster that the team created. After each spokesperson has made the presentation, the rest of the team will join him or her for a question and answer session from the teacher and classmates.

2. Have students write a paragraph tracing a new product from raw material to market.

AUTHENTIC ASSESSMENT | ACTIVITY 8

FREE TRADE

▼ BACKGROUND

Our nation's history includes arguments for and against free trade. Over the years, American trade policies have included compromises after disagreements about taxes, tariffs, and boycotted products occurred.

▼ MATERIALS

Yard-wide rolled paper (butcher paper) for time lines; marker pens; pictures and photos

▼ OBJECTIVES

After completing this activity, students will be able to

- Trace and explain the history of free trade and trade barriers.
- Describe the arguments for and against free trade and managed trade.
- Evaluate and critique tariffs from colonial America to the present.
- Evaluate if free trade has ever been really free.

PROCEDURE

1. Review and discuss global economic pressures such as the U.S. trade deficit, U.S. imports and exports, and the effect of technological advances on the global market and the U.S. economy and jobs.

2. Organize the class into three groups. Each group will be responsible for researching and making a time line of one of the following eras in the history of American global trading: colonial America to 1800, United States trade in the 1800s, and United States trade in the twentieth century. In constructing the time line, groups will add appropriate comments, pictures/photos, and symbols to illustrate the various important trade events on their portion of the time line.

3. Each group will make an oral presentation of their work, explaining the events that they have chosen to include. Some events that might be included are:

   Colonial America: Early trade routes and products, triangular trade, the slave trade, internal/external taxes, Boston Tea Party, and constitutional controversies on trade and tariffs.

   The United States in the 1800s: The Embargo Act (Jefferson's administration), Non-Intercourse Act, protective tariffs (textiles), Tariff of Abominations, Compromise of 1833, McKinley Tariff, New York Trade Fair of 1845, and the Philadelphia Centennial Exposition of 1876.

   The United States in the Twentieth Century: Payne-Aldridge Tariff, the Underwood Act, the Smoot-Hawley Act, GATT, NAFTA, and the European Union.

4. Organize the class into groups of four, two to a team, to research and hold a debate before the class on the following question: The United States should have a policy of free trade in the global economy.

5. As an enrichment activity, you may wish to have students write a paper on the topic, "Has free trade ever been free?" or write a letter to a member of the U.S. Congress expressing their viewpoint on a current trade issue (NAFTA, GATT, etc.).

◉ Assessment

1. Students will use the assessment lists for a poster and an oral presentation to evaluate their time lines.

2. Students will use the classroom assessment lists for group work and an issue controversy to evaluate their papers or letters.

3. Students will use the classroom assessment list for a writing to evaluate their papers or letters.

AUTHENTIC ASSESSMENT | ACTIVITY 9

GOVERNMENT'S ROLE IN PRICING

▼ BACKGROUND

In a free market, prices are set by the interaction of supply and demand. Sometimes, however, society has other goals besides market efficiency, such as fairness and security. To achieve these goals, government may make policies that interfere with free-market pricing.

▼ MATERIALS

Acetate transparencies and projector, flip charts, colored markers, poster board

▼ OBJECTIVES

After completing this activity, students will be able to

- Explain why government sometimes influences prices in a market.
- Describe the consequences of having a fixed price in a market.
- Understand the controversy surrounding government intervention in markets.

PROCEDURE

1. Organize the class into three groups. Assign each group one of these debate topics:

   Resolved: The government should raise the minimum wage.
   Resolved: The government should expand price supports for farmers.
   Resolved: The government should establish rent-controlled housing in all major cities.

2. Tell the groups that they will debate their assigned topic. Have the groups meet and decide which students will take the affirmative position and which will take the negative position. The two sides should have a similar number of students. These will be the debate teams.

3. Instruct the debate teams to research both sides of their issue. The teams must be able to rebut their opponents' position as well as support their own. Each team should analyze the issue by gathering information on its historical background, the main arguments for and against, and the reasons for each position. They should gather evidence, such as statistics, current or historical examples, facts, and expert opinions.

4. Debate teams should meet to prepare their arguments to support their position and rebut the opponents' position. Each team should choose two speakers—one to present the team's position and the other to rebut the opponents' position.

5. Together, each debate team should plan and prepare visuals of their evidence. Visuals may be prepared as transparencies, flip charts, posters, slides, or some other medium.

6. Hold a debate on each topic. As the two teams debate a topic, the rest of the class will serve as judges. Alternate the speakers as follows: (1) speaker supporting the affirmative position, (2) speaker supporting the negative position, (3) speaker rebutting the affirmative position, (4) speaker rebutting the negative position.

7. After both teams debate a topic, ask the rest of the class to vote on who won the debate. Then call the next group to debate the next topic.

8. When all three debates are concluded, ask the class to discuss these follow-up questions to summarize their learning: What kinds of things happen when government gets involved in setting prices? Should government set prices in some cases or leave price-setting up to the forces of supply and demand?

◉ Assessment

1. Students will use assessment lists for an issue controversy, an oral presentation, group work, and a poster or slide show, depending on the type of visuals they use.

AUTHENTIC ASSESSMENT ACTIVITY 10

CREDIT

▼ BACKGROUND

Many students will receive an invitation to use a credit card after they graduate from high school. Oil companies know students use cars, and credit card companies know they need credit. Students may also inquire about borrowing from different financial institutions, setting up charge accounts, and checking on their credit ratings. Students need to learn to make rational economic choices about credit and its uses in their personal lives and understand the importance of living within their means.

▼ MATERIALS

Teacher-collected copies of various credit offers, forms for credit, credit cards

▼ OBJECTIVES

After completing this activity, students will be able to

- Discuss the types of credit available and the institutions offering this credit.
- Understand the importance of consumer credit in the economy and their personal lives.

PROCEDURE

1. Organize the class into groups of five or less.

2. Ask each group to research a financial institution, such as a commercial bank, a savings and loan, a credit union, a finance company, or a consumer finance company to find the following information:
   a. monthly charge for checks (checking institutions)
   b. cost of checks (checking institutions)
   c. cost of a returned check (checking institutions)
   d. holding time for out-of-town checks (checking institutions)
   e. policy on two-party checks (checking institutions)
   f. ATM fees
   g. APR rates for credit cards, annual fees, and late fees

3. Ask each group to get information on charge accounts at major department stores in the area. Students might check nationally known stores such as Sears, J.C. Penney, Wal-Mart or choose one of the regionally prominent stores where they live.

4. Distribute to each group one or more credit card offers. The offers should include pertinent information about interest charges, the terms of credit, and the name of the institution. NOTE: If these are offers that were sent to individuals, be certain that the name and addresses of the people to whom they were sent are blocked out.

5. Each group will inquire about loan information from a variety of financial lending institutions. Information solicited should include what types of loans are available (purpose for the loan), how much can be borrowed in each category, the interest rates for various types of loans, the repayment schedules, and penalties for early or late payment.

6. Invite a guest speaker to explain credit ratings, credit rating systems, credit bureaus, and the significance of checking your credit rating periodically.

7. As an enrichment activity, you may wish to have students create cartoons for a bulletin board display to stimulate interest concerning uses of credit.

◉ Assessment

1. Each group will prepare a graph showing interest rates charged for credit cards.

2. Each group will write and present a three-minute skit showing the use/misuse of borrowing or the use/misuse of credit card purchasing.

AUTHENTIC ASSESSMENT · ACTIVITY 11

HOUSING AND TRANSPORTATION TRADE-OFFS

▼ BACKGROUND

Housing and transportation choices include trade-offs. It is important for students to be aware of certain factors when shopping for housing and transportation. A consumer, like a business, has to "be aware."

▼ MATERIALS

Classified advertisements for apartments and automobiles; amortization for an automobile loan for 60 months at 10 percent interest; automobile insurance rate schedules

▼ OBJECTIVES

After completing this activity, students will be able to

- Determine an estimated monthly cost of living on their own.
- Determine an estimated yearly cost of owning and operating an automobile.
- Compare costs of apartments in the local area.

PROCEDURE

1. Have the following list typed on a worksheet and hand it out to the students. Let them fill in their own numbers as you walk through it with them.

HOUSING AND TRANSPORTATION WORKSHEET

Assume that when you graduate from high school, you take a job for $10 per hour and that you work 40 hours per week. You will earn $ _____ per week. Once you deduct 15 percent for federal withholding taxes, you will take home $ _____ each week.

FILL IN THE AMOUNT OF MONEY YOU THINK YOU WILL BE SPENDING FOR THE FOLLOWING ITEMS MONTHLY

1. Rent _____   2. Utilities _____   3. Telephone _____
4. Car payment _____   5. Gas, oil, maintenance, tires _____   6. Insurance _____
7. Food _____   8. Laundry _____   9. Personal items _____
                                                    (deodorant, hairspray, etc.)
10. Entertainment _____   TOTAL _____

2. Have students use the classified ads to find an apartment to rent and record the price. Then have them use the ads to find a car to buy.

   a. Have them find a car in the newspaper that they like and write down the price. Now add about $500 for tax, title, and license. Ask them to record this price as well.

   b. Have them calculate the monthly payments on a car loan at 10 percent interest by the using the amortization schedule.

   c. Have students calculate their maintenance costs per month by assuming that they use 12 gallons of gas weekly at $2.90 per gallon and that they get their oil changed every three months for $25.

   d. Have them calculate their insurance rates by referring to the insurance tables.

◉ Assessment

1. Organize the class into groups of four. Ask each group to discuss their worksheets and brainstorm ideas of how to decrease their monthly costs. Are there ways that they could increase their incomes?

2. Have each group come up with a composite budget to present to the class, along with their suggestions for either increasing their income or decreasing their expenses.

AUTHENTIC ASSESSMENT   ACTIVITY 12

PUBLIC GOODS

▼ **BACKGROUND**

Public goods are products collectively consumed by everyone. Use by one person does not reduce the satisfaction or value of the goods to others. A market economy does not provide these goods because they are not profitable. As a result, government usually supplies them.

▼ **MATERIALS**

Word processing or desktop publishing software, Internet access if possible, printer

▼ **OBJECTIVES**

After completing this activity, students will be able to
- Understand the nature of public goods.
- Discuss current issues involving public goods.
- Identify consequences of government decisions concerning public goods.

RUBRICS

newspaper article, group work

PROCEDURE

1. Write the following five topics on the chalkboard: government clean air standards, oil drilling on public wildlife preserves, budget for military spending, businesses that release toxic wastes into streams or lakes, logging in national parks. Ask the class to identify the public goods associated with each topic. (*in topic order: clean air, preservation of wildlife, national defense, clean water, national parks*) Write the public goods on the chalkboard next to the appropriate topic.

2. Organize the class into pairs of students. Explain that each pair will write a two-page newspaper article on one of these topics. Have the pairs confer and choose a topic. Try to have each topic covered by at least one pair.

3. Instruct the pairs to research current events related to their topic. Advise them to collect facts and quotations from several online or print publications. They might find quotes from government officials, interest-group spokespeople, and experts in the field. They should also download or scan pictures to help illustrate their article. Instruct them to make photocopies or printouts of their sources to submit with their articles.

4. Ask partners to meet as needed to plan their article. Suggest that each pair follow these planning steps:
   - Evaluate the information that each collected.
   - Choose a focus or theme for the article and create an outline.
   - Select facts and quotations to use.
   - Write the article and obtain feedback from their partners.
   - Revise based on the feedback.
   - Choose illustrations and write captions.
   - Write an attention-grabbing headline.
   - Prepare the final draft in a word processing or desktop publishing program, paring it down as needed to fill no more than two pages.

5. Have each pair display their finished article on the bulletin board. Ask them to submit copies of their sources to you.

6. Allow time for students to read the articles produced by the other pairs.

◉ Assessment

1. Students will use the classroom assessment lists for a newspaper article and group work.

AUTHENTIC ASSESSMENT — ACTIVITY 13

L ABOR

▼ BACKGROUND

The labor movement has tried to organize workers to deal with management more efficiently and to settle disagreements through negotiations rather than through work stoppages.

▼ MATERIALS

Copies of the scenario of Farris Meats

▼ OBJECTIVES

After completing this activity, students will be able to

- Define collective bargaining, mediation, and arbitration.
- Examine the impact of unions and strikes on management and labor.

PROCEDURE

1. Organize the class into groups of six. Each group should have three members representing management and three representing labor who are to negotiate a new union contract. The current contract states:

   a. All workers receive $9 per hour for a 45-hour workweek that includes 30 minutes for lunch each day.

   b. Each worker may take two days of sick leave per year.

   c. The company pays $25 of each worker's $130 health-insurance premium each month.

   d. Workers may take two weeks unpaid vacation each year.

   Management wants to keep the same contract. The workers want to improve pay, working conditions, and benefits.

2. Have the groups negotiate for about 15 minutes and write up a contract. Use the negotiations as the basis for a class discussion on collective bargaining and other tactics used in negotiations.

3. Distribute copies of the following scenario to each of the groups. Let them read the scenario and answer the questions. For each choice, they should give possible effects on both labor and management.

SCENARIO

Suppose the economy is in a recession and jobs are hard to find. Some large corporations, however, are making large profits. Farris Meats, one of the leading meatpackers in the United States, is doing extremely well. Assume that Farris Meats has a factory in your hometown of Faithful. Faithful has a population of about 10,000 and at least 4,000 of those work at the Farris factory. In one month, the current contract at the factory will expire. Rumor has it that Farris intends to cut wages from $11 an hour to $10 an hour in only the Faithful factory. All of the 4,000 workers at the factory belong to a national union of meatpackers. The local chapter in Faithful wants to go on strike, so they contact the national union officials to drum support for their strike. When contract negotiations begin one month later, management will not budge. What would happen if:

a. the local union in Faithful strikes without support of their national union?

b. Farris picks up the slack in the other factories and closes the Faithful factory?

c. the national union supports the local union in Faithful?

d. the local union goes on strike without the support of the national union and the Farris Company tells the local union that they have three months to go back to work or they will be replaced permanently?

e. against national union advice, some other workers in other cities go on a sympathy strike?

◉ Assessment

1. Have students do a research paper on a historical or current labor dispute.

AUTHENTIC ASSESSMENT   ACTIVITY 14

TAXES

▼ BACKGROUND

Government needs an enormous amount of money to operate, and most of this money comes from taxes. Taxes may not always seem fair to everyone. However, taxes are necessary to provide the goods and services we all need and want, but cannot afford to provide for ourselves.

▼ MATERIALS

None

▼ OBJECTIVES

After completing this activity, students will be able to

• Identify the types of taxes and their impact.
• Evaluate taxes in terms of fairness.

PROCEDURE

1. Organize students into four groups. Assign each group a level of government to research (federal, state, local, or community). Have each group contact the tax-collection agency, such as the IRS or county tax assessor, for their level of government.

2. Have students further divide their groups into two teams and have one team find the answers to the following questions:

   • What types of taxes make up your sources of revenue?
   • What percentage of your total revenues come from each source?
   • How would you classify each tax—progressive, regressive, or proportional?

   Have the other team find the answers to these questions:

   • What are the government's expenses?
   • What percentage of your revenues goes for each expenditure?
   • Are certain revenues used for specific expenditures? Specify.

3. Have each team use the information it gathers to create a circle graph. The circle graphs made by the first teams should show where government revenues come from. Suggest that the teams color the sections of the graphs to indicate the kinds of taxes they represent. For example, all sections standing for regressive taxes might be colored blue. The graphs made by the second teams should show where government revenues go. Suggest that they color code their sections to show which taxes pay for what.

4. Have groups meet to study the circle graphs each team created for their levels of government. Each member should choose a tax and find reasons, based on the graphs, to explain why they think that tax is fair or unfair.

⦿ Assessment

1. Have each of the four groups use their circle graphs as visual aids and give an oral presentation explaining their findings to the class.

2. As homework, have the students redo their team's circle graph as if government has eliminated the tax or taxes that each student considers unfair.

AUTHENTIC ASSESSMENT | ACTIVITY 15

GOVERNMENTAL BUDGETS

▼ BACKGROUND

Considerable debate and compromise are necessary to prepare an annual governmental budget. Because all resources are scarce, an increase in spending in one area will either increase debt or decrease spending in another area.

▼ MATERIALS

Compasses, protractors, markers, calculators, and poster board

▼ OBJECTIVES

After completing this activity, students will be able to

- Understand the need for compromise when creating a government budget.
- Adjust a budget to accommodate changes in people's needs.

PROCEDURE

1. On the chalkboard, copy the following table showing expenditures by a state government.

State Expenditures	Millions of Dollars	Percent of Total
General Government	1,238	3.5
Education	13,416	38.3
Employee Benefits	1,618	4.6
Health and Human Services	12,005	34.3
Public Safety and Corrections	1,938	5.5
Transportation	2,726	7.8
Natural Resources and Recreational Services	589	1.7
Regulatory Agencies	169	0.5
Debt Service	348	1.0
Agricultural Development	999	2.8
Total Expenditures	35,046	100.0

2. Organize the class into small groups. They are responsible for creating a state budget for next year. The state total budget and expenditures is $35,046,000,000. Distribute the following scenarios to each group:

- The state has promised to put a computer in every classroom, at a cost of $50 million.
- The state oil industry goes into a slump, and the state loses $130 million in state revenues.
- Activists pressure the state to buy and protect four million acres of private forestland at a cost of $500 million.
- State employees demand a 30% increase in benefits ($485 million more) to cover the rise in the cost of living.
- Human Services has asked for $200 million more for the state's 1.1 million children living in poverty.

3. Tell groups to assume that state revenues are the same unless otherwise indicated in the scenario.

4. Ask each group to make a poster-sized circle graph showing the state's budget for next year.

⦿ Assessment

1. Have each group appoint a speaker to explain the budget changes to the rest of the class.

2. Ask each student to draw a political cartoon commenting on one of the budget changes.

AUTHENTIC ASSESSMENT — ACTIVITY 16

THE FUNCTIONS AND CHARACTERISTICS OF MONEY

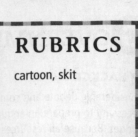

RUBRICS

cartoon, skit

▼ BACKGROUND

Money makes it possible for businesses and consumers to obtain goods.

▼ MATERIALS

10 pictures of various items from catalogs (large enough to be seen from the back of the room and pasted on cardboard) with prices written on the back of each picture

▼ OBJECTIVES

After completing this activity, students will be able to
- Determine the characteristics of money.
- Describe the functions of money.

PROCEDURE

1. Put the pictures on the chalkboard in random order. Have the students, first as individuals, determine the order of value, choosing number 1 as the most valuable and number 10 as the least valuable. Have them also try to guess how much each good costs.

2. Then, as a class, they should put the products in order, again from most valuable to least valuable. Once they have come to a consensus on the order, let them decide as a class the price of each item.

3. Ask the students what a minimum wage is, and have one student calculate the number of hours someone would have to work to earn each of these items. Ask them how many of them would be willing to work for "x" amount of hours for these items. How many would be willing to receive the same items each time they worked the required number of hours? (Obviously, they are not willing to do this. Ask: Why not? Eventually, money will come into the discussion.)

4. Discuss with students that they have just illustrated two of the functions of money: a standard of value (the price helped them determine how valuable items were) and a medium of exchange (they were not willing to work that same number of hours for the same products; thereby money allows both the buyer and the seller something on which they can agree).

5. Go on to discuss the characteristics of money (divisibility, durability, acceptability, and portability).

◉ Assessment

1. Have students draw cartoons that illustrate functions and characteristics of money.

2. Have students present skits that would illustrate life without money, or what life would be like if money did not have the characteristics it has.

AUTHENTIC ASSESSMENT — ACTIVITY 17

THE STOCK MARKET

▼ BACKGROUND

The largest volume of over-the-counter stock transactions takes place through the National Association of Securities Dealers Automated Quotations (NASDAQ) system.

▼ MATERIALS

Copies of a portion of the NASDAQ for four consecutive days, or four consecutive Fridays; calculators

▼ OBJECTIVES

After completing this activity, students will be able to

• Read the stock market listings in their local newspaper.

• Calculate potential gains and losses in stock transactions.

PROCEDURE

1. Organize the class into pairs of students. Tell students to suppose that they each have $10,000 to invest in their own "stock portfolios." Then give them copies of the earliest NASDAQ quotations in your set of four. Explain that the letters on each line stand for a company's name. The figures under *Vol.* (volume) are the amounts of shares in the company that were bought and sold on that day. The figures under *Close* are the prices of the stocks at the end of the day. Those are the amounts they will pay for shares. (To change the fractional amounts to a decimal, divide the numerator by the denominator and write the answer as a decimal.) The figures under *Chg.* are the amounts that the stock prices went up (+) or down (-) since the beginning of the trading day. Have students choose companies that look promising and decide how many shares of each to buy for their portfolios.

2. Have students keep a journal of their stock transactions. Tell them to copy the date from the NASDAQ quotation at the start of their entry. Then have them record the name of each stock that they bought, the number of shares, the price per share, the reasons they chose the stock, and how much of their $10,000 they spent. For each company they invest in, remind them to deduct $40 in fees. However, if they buy more than 100 shares in a company's stock, they get a discount and pay only $30 in fees for that trade. Also, ask each student to set a goal, such as a 1% profit at the end of the four "trading sessions."

3. Distribute the second set of NASDAQ quotations. Have students check the progress of the stocks they bought and decide whether to sell all, some, or none their shares. If they have money left to invest, encourage them to buy more shares of stocks. Remind them to record the details of their transactions, including their gains or losses after selling stock.

4. Repeat the process for the last two sets of NASDAQ quotations. Then have students figure out their gains or losses over the four "trading sessions" and add this information to their last journal entry.

◉ Assessment

1. Have students assess their own performance, including the percent of change in the value of their portfolios. Remember, percent of change = amount of change divided by the initial investment. Then have students list what actions they would repeat when selling and buying stocks and how they would improve their trading in the future.

2. Instruct students to write newspaper articles relating their experiences with the pleasures and perils of trading in the stock market.

AUTHENTIC ASSESSMENT — ACTIVITY 18

ECONOMIC INDICATORS

▼ BACKGROUND

Economic indicators measure economic variables, such as the dollar amount of loans to be repaid. Leading indicators predict the direction of an economy, coincident indicators signal the beginning of changes, and lagging indicators give clues to economists about the phases of the business cycle.

▼ OBJECTIVES

After completing this activity, students will be able to

- Classify economic indicators into three broad categories.
- Calculate economic changes that students experience as a class.

▼ MATERIALS

Calculators

PROCEDURE

1. Tell students that some major economic indicators, such as number of employed workers, average length of unemployment, and number of loans to be repaid, may have parallels in their own class-size economy. Write a list of indicators on the chalkboard.

2. Have students categorize each indicator as Leading Indicator, Coincident Indicator, or Lagging Indicator.

3. Survey the class using the form that follows. Have each student anonymously fill in a table with the number of hours worked at a job during each month, the amount of income earned each month, and how much debt they had each month. Collect all the tables, average the numbers for the class as a whole, and have students calculate the percent of change from the month before. Record this data on a copy of the same form, labeling it as the class average.

Leading Indicators	Sept	Oct	Nov	Dec	Jan	Feb	March
Number of hours worked							
Percent change							
Coincident Indicators							
Income*							
Percent change							
Lagging Indicators							
Indebtedness							
Percent change							

*salaries and allowances

4. Organize the students into groups. Have each group develop an explanation for the changes in the chart.

◉ Assessment

1. Have students make a bulletin board based on the chart, with an added column of explanations.

2. Tell each student to draw a line graph that shows the changes for one or more indicators.

AUTHENTIC ASSESSMENT | ACTIVITY 19

INFLATION

▼ BACKGROUND

Rising and falling prices affect the value of the dollar both domestically and abroad. Controlling inflation increases the purchasing power of American consumers.

▼ MATERIALS

Play money; two or three bags of small candies (various kinds); a couple of large candy bars

▼ OBJECTIVES

After completing this activity, students will be able to

- Define inflation.
- State the effects inflation has on people in various economic positions.
- List some negative and positive effects of inflation.

PROCEDURE

1. Organize the class into buyers and sellers. Give the sellers one piece of candy to sell. Be sure to give each seller a different kind so that the buyers will have some choices. Give each of the buyers a one dollar bill. You can give some of the buyers more than one bill, but give out only a total of 10 bills. Let them buy and sell for about one minute. In round 2, give each seller one piece of candy, again different kinds, but now to increase the money supply, give out about 40 bills. Let them buy and sell for one minute. Be sure to tell the sellers that the seller with the most money will be able to purchase a large candy bar at the end of the round.

2. Discuss what happened in round 2. (*The price of the candy went up because there was more money in circulation. This is called* DEMAND-PULL *inflation—too much money chasing too few goods.*)

3. Ask: Is inflation good or bad? If so, for whom?

4. Write this list on the chalkboard:

   a. union worker in a clothing factory
   b. loan officer in a bank
   c. married couple buying a house
   d. retired schoolteacher
   e. homeowner with a high-interest mortgage
   f. car owner with a low-interest loan

5. Organize the class into six groups. Have each group select one of the classifications above and write a description of how continuing inflation might affect the person's standard of living or business operation.

6. Have a representative from each group read the descriptions aloud and poll the class for accuracy.

7. Discuss the good and bad effects of inflation on people of various incomes. Ask: Does anyone benefit?

8. Have them list as a class some products they have purchased recently whose prices have gone up. Brainstorm with the class possible reasons for the price increases. Conclude the activity by discussing cost-push inflation. This might lead you into a discussion about OPEC, technology, or productivity.

◉ Assessment

1. Have each student choose a product and use CPI statistics to graph inflation for his or her product.

2. Have students draw a cartoon illustrating either cost-push or demand-pull inflation.

3. Have students write a song about the effects of inflation.

AUTHENTIC ASSESSMENT   ACTIVITY 20

FISCAL AND MONETARY POLICIES

▼ BACKGROUND

One of the most important responsibilities of the Federal Reserve is to control the money supply through monetary policy, thereby influencing economic activity. Fiscal policy, which is carried out by Congress, is also a way to control economic activity.

▼ MATERIALS

One poster board with a large circle graph that includes the following 10 divisions: raise the reserve requirement, lower the reserve requirement, raise the discount rate, lower the discount rate, sell bonds, buy bonds, increase expenditures, decrease expenditures, raise taxes, and lower taxes; a tongue depressor mounted as a spinner on the graph; six other poster boards; assorted markers

▼ OBJECTIVES

After completing this activity, students will be able to

- Describe how monetary and fiscal policies affect bankers, consumers, and businesses.
- Understand the tools the government uses to conduct monetary and fiscal policies.

PROCEDURE

1. Explain to the class the difference between monetary and fiscal policies, including who makes each policy and why.

2. Choose one student to represent the federal government. The student's job is simply to spin the tongue depressor on the poster board with the circle graph and call out the federal policy the depressor points to.

3. Organize the class into three groups. Each group will represent one of the following: bankers, consumers, and businesses. Have the groups first write down the call of the spin on the circle graph and then decide what effect the call will have on them. *(Bankers would be concerned about money available to loan. Consumers would be concerned with money to borrow and spend and job losses because of economic downturns. Businesses would be concerned about money to borrow, available cash for consumers, and inventory.)*

◉ Assessment

1. Organize the class into six new groups, making certain that each group includes at least one banker, one consumer, and one business. Together, they will make a "chain reaction" display illustrating what happened with each call in the previous round. They can add pictures if they wish, but the display must show the call, then the effect on the bank, the consumer, and the business, in that order.

2. Each group must display at least three calls.

AUTHENTIC ASSESSMENT | ACTIVITY 21

Economic STABILITY

▼ BACKGROUND

The Employment Act of 1946 clearly states the federal government's commitment to stabilizing the economy: "The Congress hereby declares that it is the continuing policy and responsibility of the Federal Government . . . to promote maximum employment, production, and purchasing power."

▼ OBJECTIVES

After completing this activity, students will be able to
- Recognize government actions that affect the economy's stability.
- Analyze the effects of government decisions on the economy.

▼ MATERIALS

Recent newspapers, news magazines, almanacs, and federal publications

PROCEDURE

1. Have students conduct a trial to decide whether the federal government has kept its promises to stabilize the economy. First, list these promises from the above excerpt on the chalkboard:
   - to promote maximum employment
   - to promote maximum production
   - to promote maximum purchasing power

   Distribute recent newspapers, news magazines, almanacs, and federal publications. Direct students to look for articles that discuss the government and the economy.

2. Have a "defense attorney" meet with five or six "witnesses" with articles that show that the government keeps the promises listed on the chalkboard. Have a "prosecuting attorney" meet with five or six "witnesses" with articles that suggest that government actions undermine the economy's stability. Instruct each group to prepare a skit portraying a lawyer questioning friendly witnesses.

3. Have students conduct the trial. Suggest that attorneys ad-lib questions for hostile witnesses and objections such as "Hearsay" and that a student "judge" sustain or overrule the objections.

4. Have nonparticipants act as "jurors" to decide which side is more convincing.

◉ Assessment

1. Have players as well as jurors evaluate the skits.

2. Ask each juror to assess the performances of each "side."

AUTHENTIC ASSESSMENT — ACTIVITY 22

TRADE AND INTERDEPENDENCE

RUBRICS

research report, graph, poster

▼ BACKGROUND

International trade has become increasingly important as our world resources diminish.

▼ MATERIALS

Products with labels showing where they were manufactured (displayed on a table), construction paper (red, green, yellow, white, and blue—six full pieces of each color), three pairs of scissors, two glue-sticks, a ruler, a pencil

▼ OBJECTIVES

After completing this activity, students will be able to

- Define interdependence.
- Understand how scarcity promotes the need to trade.

PROCEDURE

1. Have the students examine the products on display. Have them call out the names of the places where these items were made. Write the word *interdependence* on the chalkboard.

2. Write the following list on the chalkboard:

   1. A 4-inch × 4-inch red square
   2. 4 yellow strips, 3 inches × 1 inch
   3. A green four-leaf clover
   4. A blue diamond, 4 inches long
   5. A 3-inch blue star with a white circle attached to each point
   6. A white square, 6 inches × 6 inches, with a red triangle attached as a roof
   7. A bound book made of three colors, with writing on each page
   8. A white flag, 6 inches × 4 inches, with 5 blue stars and 7 red stripes
   9. A 5-inch Christmas tree with a yellow star attached to the top and 10 blue triangles attached to the tree
   10. Five $1 bills

3. Organize the class into five groups. Give the groups the materials listed below in an envelope. Tell them the object of the game is to produce as many of the items on the chalkboard as possible. Explain that if they do not have what they need, they will have to come to the bargaining table and trade.

   MATERIALS

   GROUP 1: Two sheets of red, green, and blue paper; a pair of scissors; a ruler; a glue-stick; and a pencil

   GROUP 2: Two sheets of white, yellow, and green paper; two $1 bills; and scissors

   GROUP 3: Two sheets of yellow and white paper; nine $1 bills; and a pencil

   GROUP 4: Two sheets of white, red, and blue paper; two $1 bills; a glue-stick; and a pair of scissors

   GROUP 5: One sheet of red, green, yellow, and blue paper; and seven $1 bills

4. Let the students attempt to finish the tasks for about 25 minutes.

5. Discuss with the class how economic concepts apply to world trade.

◉ Assessment

1. Have each student select a European country. Have them find out how many American businesses have offices in that country, research what products we import from the country, and make a chart.

2. Have students use their research on a European country to write a paper on the true meaning of interdependence.

AUTHENTIC ASSESSMENT — ACTIVITY 23

POVERTY IN AMERICA

▼ BACKGROUND

The United States is a wealthy nation, yet the wealth is not spread evenly. Millions of Americans live in poverty. The government sponsors programs to help those in need. The president and Congress choose the types of programs and their funding.

▼ MATERIALS

Poster board, colored markers, dowel sticks, glue for mounting signs

▼ OBJECTIVES

After completing this activity, students will be able to
- Analyze factors that contribute to poverty in America.
- Understand how poverty affects individuals and families.
- Describe government programs designed to fight poverty.

RUBRICS

skit, group work, poster

PROCEDURE

1. Write the following list on the board. Ask students to contribute more ideas about why some individuals and families are living in poverty. Add their ideas to the list.

CONDITIONS CONTRIBUTING TO POVERTY

- structural change in the economy
- lack of job skills
- single-parenthood
- illness of family member
- discrimination
- elderly with no savings
- layoffs
- disability

2. Organize the class into groups of four or five. Instruct the students as follows:

- You are members of a group seeking to improve conditions for the poor. All of you are people living in poverty but for different reasons. Congress is holding a hearing on poverty to decide what programs to fund. Your representative has asked your group to testify at the hearing. Each of you will play a character who testifies at the hearing.
- Meet with your small group. Together, assign one reason from the list on the chalkboard to each group member. Each member should have a different reason.
- Individually, research your reason and programs that could help. Write a brief personal story your character will tell at the hearing. End with a suggestion for how the government should spend its funds to help you. Be prepared to answer questions from Congress about your problems and suggested solution.
- Each individual should create a sign to carry to the hearing. The sign should state in a few words or with visuals the main point your character wants Congress to consider.

3. Have the groups give you their characters' names in advance. Call the first group to the front of the class with their signs. Call each character by name to give their story. The rest of the class serves as Congress. Have them ask each character one or two questions. After one group testifies, call the next.

4. End with a class discussion of what students learned about poverty from the activity.

◉ Assessment

1. Students will use the classroom assessment lists for a skit, group work, and a poster.

AUTHENTIC ASSESSMENT — ACTIVITY 24

ECONOMIC GROWTH IN DEVELOPING COUNTRIES

▼ BACKGROUND

A major indicator of growth in a developing nation's economy is improvements in the well-being of its children.

▼ MATERIALS

Access to the Internet and desktop publishing programs

▼ OBJECTIVES

After completing this activity, students will be able to

- Specify economy-related issues concerning children in developing nations.
- Identify ways developed nations can help children in developing nations.

PROCEDURE

1. Organize the class into five groups. Assign each group a region—Latin America and the Caribbean, the Middle East and North Africa, Africa south of the Sahara, South Asia, or East Asia and the Pacific. Have each member research a children's issue in the region's developing nations.

2. Explain to students that the United Nation's Children's Fund (UNICEF) has a statistical yardstick called the Child Risk Measure (CRM) that is based in part on economy-related factors such as prevalence of HIV/AIDS in children, underweight children, under-five mortality, primary school attendance, and immunization against major diseases such as polio. Suggest that students find information about these issues at the UNICEF Web site at *http://www.unicefusa.org* or by writing to United States Committee for UNICEF, 125 Maiden Lane, New York, NY 10038. (Note: If students write to UNICEF for information, they should include stamped, self-addressed envelopes with their requests.)

3. Point out that students should also consider ways to fund improvements in the lives of children. For example, one UNICEF report notes that Africa south of the Sahara spends more on servicing its $200 billion debt than on the health and education of its children; therefore, the report calls on developed nations to cancel these debts to developing nations.

◉ Assessment

1. Have each group create a booklet describing the children's issues in its region.

2. Ask students to write persuasive letters to their U.S. senators or representatives championing a specific way that developed nations can help children in developing nations.

AUTHENTIC ASSESSMENT   ACTIVITY 25

THE GLOBAL ECONOMY

▼ BACKGROUND

Every day Americans come into contact with goods and services that are directly or indirectly related to people around the world. We trade globally, travel globally, and communicate globally and, thus, our lives are touched frequently by international goods, services, and ideas.

▼ MATERIALS

Newspapers, such as the Wall Street Journal, with a daily listing of foreign exchange rates; old newspapers and magazines that can be cut up; poster board or corrugated board from shipping boxes that can be used as mounting material; scissors and glue

▼ OBJECTIVES

After completing this activity, students will be able to

- Identify a variety of consumer goods from foreign markets.
- Survey and record the foreign-made merchandise in their own homes.
- Explain the different currencies of the world and their relationship to one another.

PROCEDURE

1. Organize the class into five groups for a scavenger hunt.

2. Assign each group to a different area of each group member's home (for example: kitchen/pantry, living room/family room, bath/bedroom, den/office/spare room, garage/storage/laundry.)

3. Each student in the group should be responsible for recording a minimum of five foreign-made or partially foreign-made items in the assigned area. Each student should compile a list that identifies the name of the item (stereo, T.V., sweater, automobile, appliance, etc.) and describe it sufficiently so that its cost may be estimated. The list should also note each item's country of origin where possible.

4. When the students have completed their inventories, they should bring the results back to the group and estimate the cost of each identified item. Using the newspaper, the group should convert the estimated cost in dollars to the foreign exchange rate for the country of origin.

5. Each group will create a collage of the items found in the scavenger hunt of their homes by cutting up newspapers and magazines and gluing pictures and letters to the mounting boards. If pictures cannot be found of items surveyed, then students should cut out letters and spell out the item.

6. Each group will present an oral review of the products found in the scavenger hunt of their homes, identifying the countries of origin, and stating the estimated value of each item in dollars and the appropriate foreign currency.

7. As an enrichment activity, you may wish to have students make a slide show or a photo essay showing global products with maps identifying countries of origin. Students should discuss these countries' trade policies and contrast American versions of the same goods (if any) by comparing price differentials using foreign exchange conversion charts. Methods for converting the various currencies at current exchange rates should be included in the presentation. This could be a group or individual effort.

⊙ Assessment

1. Students will make collages of foreign-made goods and their prices and explain these collages to the class.

2. Students will use classroom assessment lists for an oral presentation, group work, a poster, and a slide show or photo essay.

Authentic Assessment Activities

RUBRIC

A Booklet or Pamphlet

S: This work goes beyond the rating of **T.** It is especially eloquent.

T: Overall, this work is excellent. It accomplishes its purpose and communicates well with the intended audience. There is a clear, focused theme for the whole piece and each component supports it. There is a controlled, logical sequence with a clear plan for the entire piece and for each of its components. The supporting details enhance the quality of the main ideas and they are woven into the work and do not seem "stuck on" or list-like. Accurate and appropriate information from a variety of sources is used in the proper quantity and in the proper locations. The sources are properly referenced. The author's own thinking is clearly evident. Diagrams, pictures, and other graphics are of high technical quality, making the text clearer and more interesting. The proper format is used throughout. There are very few, if any, mechanical errors, none of which interfere with the meaning. The work is neat and presentable.

U: This work is generally as good as that receiving a rating of **T,** but it is uneven with some relatively less-developed areas.

V: This work is generally similar to that receiving a rating of **W,** but it has one or two areas that are relatively well developed.

W: This work is weak. It does not accomplish its purpose well nor does it communicate effectively with the intended audience. The theme for the entire piece is not clear. The components do not support the theme well. The entire piece is not well organized. The components seem "stuck on" or list-like. Supporting details are lacking and/or inaccurate. It is not clear that the student understands the core curriculum related to this project. Sources are not well referenced. The author's own thinking is not evident. Diagrams, pictures, or other graphics are of poor technical quality and do not add much clarity or interest. The proper format is not used. The work contains errors that interfere with the meaning. The work is not neat and presentable.

X: This work is extremely weak in most or all areas.

CLASSROOM ASSESSMENT LIST

A Booklet or Pamphlet

Element	Assessment Points	
	Possible	**Earned**
1. There is a clear theme throughout the booklet or pamphlet.	_____	_____
2. Chapters or sections are organized to support the theme.	_____	_____
3. Chapters or sections have clear main ideas.	_____	_____
4. Main ideas are supported with appropriate information.	_____	_____
5. It is clear that the student thoroughly understands the core concepts relevant to this assignment.	_____	_____
6. The student's own thinking is clearly evident.	_____	_____
7. Information sources are properly referenced.	_____	_____
8. Diagrams, pictures, and other graphics are of high technical quality and add to the overall effectiveness of the booklet or pamphlet.	_____	_____
9. The proper format is followed.	_____	_____
10. Writing mechanics are of high quality.	_____	_____
11. The work is very neat and presentable.	_____	_____
12. The work communicates well with the intended audience.	_____	_____
13. The work is creative and interesting.	_____	_____
Total	_____	_____

RUBRIC

A Bulletin Board

S: The student has made a bulletin board that is outstanding. It is so attractive, creative, interesting, and compelling that the audience will enjoy seeing it over and over again. The message comes across very strongly. The artistic and technical aspects of the bulletin board are eloquent.

T: The student has made a bulletin board that immediately catches your eye through the use of humor, design, or other similar strategies. The message is clear and the information presented is appropriate and accurate regarding the concepts to be conveyed. The design is simple and effective. The bulletin board does not seem too full or unorganized. The mix of words, statements, and other graphics is effective. The bulletin board is very neat and presentable.

U: The bulletin board is like one that receives a rating of **T,** except there are one or two important elements that are not well done.

V: The bulletin board is like one that receives a rating of **W,** except there are one or two important elements that are well done.

W: The student has made a bulletin board that is not very interesting. The message that is intended to be conveyed is not clear. Information is missing or incorrect regarding the concepts to be conveyed. The design is cluttered and unorganized. The mix of words, statements, and other graphics does not help to accomplish the purpose of the bulletin board. The bulletin board is not neat and presentable.

X: The bulletin board is very poorly done.

CLASSROOM ASSESSMENT LIST

A Bulletin Board

Element	Assessment Points	
	Possible	**Earned**
1. The bulletin board has a clear and distinct message.	_____	_____
2. The bulletin board catches your attention through humor, design, or other similar strategy.	_____	_____
3. The information presented is appropriate and accurate regarding the concepts presented.	_____	_____
4. The design is simple and effective. It is not cluttered or confused.	_____	_____
5. The mix of words, statements, and graphics is effective.	_____	_____
6. The bulletin board has the desired effect on the intended audience.	_____	_____
7. The bulletin board is neat and presentable.	_____	_____
Total	_____	_____

RUBRIC

A Cartoon

S: The cartoon is extremely clever and humorous. The cartoon does a remarkable job of combining the elements of design with the information in the message to communicate in a powerful way with the intended audience.

T: The student has created a cartoon with a clear story line that flows from frame to frame. The character(s) is/are interesting and/or humorous. The dialogue contained in the speech and/or thought balloons provides humor and sends the appropriate message to the intended audience. The use of background context and color adds to the cartoon. The cartoon is neat and presentable. Overall, the cartoon does an excellent job of catching the audience's attention and sending an appropriate message.

U: The cartoon is generally like those receiving a rating of **T,** except there are some important elements that are not excellent. Therefore, the cartoon is unevenly excellent.

V: The cartoon is generally like those receiving a rating of **W,** except there are some important elements that are well done.

W: The student has created a cartoon that has an unclear or uneven or confusing story line. The characters are either not interesting or humorous or are inappropriate for the subject and audience. The dialogue contained in the speech and/or thought balloons does not convey the message well and/or is inappropriate to the audience. The background does not add to and may even distract from the message of the cartoon. Color is not used well. The cartoon is not neat and presentable. Overall, the cartoon does not convey the message to the intended audience well.

X: The work is very poor.

CLASSROOM ASSESSMENT LIST
A Cartoon

Element	Assessment Points	
	Possible	**Earned**
1. The story line is clear and interesting.	_____	_____
2. There is a smooth flow from one frame to the next.	_____	_____
3. The character(s) is/are interesting and/or humorous.	_____	_____
4. The dialogue in speech or thought balloons supports the story line and uses appropriate vocabulary.	_____	_____
5. The story line provides a clear message to the intended audience.	_____	_____
6. The use of background context adds to the cartoon.	_____	_____
7. The use of color enhances the cartoon.	_____	_____
8. The cartoon is neat and presentable.	_____	_____
Total	_____	_____

RUBRIC

A Display

S: The display is eye-catching and conveys a strong message immediately. The physical objects are particularly well suited to the theme. The graphics are done with great artistic and technical skill. There is neither too much nor too little in the display. The whole display works to communicate with the intended audience.

T: The student has selected a theme for the display that is very appropriate for the concepts to be conveyed. The student has selected and arranged the physical objects so that the theme is clearly carried out. Graphics, including symbols, words, statements, and designs, help carry out the theme and add interest to the display. There is a creative and thoughtful organization and coordination of the physical objects and the graphics. The display is very neat and presentable. It accomplishes its intended purpose with the target audience.

U: The display is like one that receives a rating of **T,** except there are some elements that are not excellent.

V: The display is like one that receives a rating of **W,** except there are some elements that are well done.

W: The theme selected is not very appropriate to the concepts to be conveyed. The selection and organization of physical objects show little thought and effort. The graphics are incomplete or inaccurate and do little to carry out the theme. The display is not neat and presentable. The display does not accomplish its purpose with the intended audience.

X: The display is very poorly done.

Note: If an oral presentation (taped or live) accompanies the display, it can be assessed using the rubric and classroom list for an oral presentation. If a written explanation of the display is made, it can be assessed using the rubric and classroom list for a writing.

CLASSROOM ASSESSMENT LIST

A Display

Element	Assessment Points	
	Possible	**Earned**
1. The display has a clear theme that is appropriate to the concepts being conveyed.	_____	_____
2. The physical objects in the display are well coordinated with the theme.	_____	_____
3. The graphics such as symbols, words, statements, colors, patterns, and designs help carry out the theme.	_____	_____
4. There is a clear, creative, and thoughtful organization and coordination between physical objects and the graphics in the display.	_____	_____
5. The display is attractive and presentable.	_____	_____
Total	_____	_____

Note: If an oral presentation (taped or live) accompanies the display, it can be assessed using the rubric and classroom list for an oral presentation. If a written explanation of the display is made, it can be assessed using the rubric and classroom list for a writing.

RUBRIC

A Graph

S: The student's graph is outstanding in its ability to clearly and easily convey accurate information to the reader. The graph is very interesting. The written summary is concise and accurate.

T: The student has organized data into appropriate pairs in a chart and selected the appropriate type of graph for that data. The variables are put on the correct axes, which are accurately labeled. An appropriate scale with reasonable starting points and intervals is used on each axis so that the graph uses the allotted space well. The data are plotted accurately and trend(s), or lack of it (them), is (are) accurately indicated. The title is clear and describes the two variables well. Techniques such as color, texture, or labels are used so that the graph can be read at a glance. A clear key is presented. The graph is very neat and presentable. The written summary uses appropriate language to concisely and accurately describe the relationship between the independent and dependent variables.

U: The graph is like one receiving a rating of **T,** except there are one or two important elements that are not excellent.

V: The graph is like one receiving a rating of **W,** except there are one or two important elements that are well done.

W: The data are not well organized in preparation for the graph. The incorrect type of graph was chosen. The variables are plotted on the wrong axes. The axes are not labeled or labeled inadequately. The scales used are not appropriate and the lines or bars do not use the space of the graph well. The title is missing or inadequate. Techniques such as color, texture, or labels are not used well to enhance the ease of interpretation of the graph. The key is missing or inadequate. The written summary does not accurately and/or clearly describe the relationship between the two variables.

X: The graph is very poorly done.

CLASSROOM ASSESSMENT LIST

A Graph

Element	Assessment Points	
	Possible	**Earned**

1. In preparation for the graph, data pairs are organized into a labeled chart. _____ _____

2. The appropriate type of graph is used. _____ _____

3. The independent variable is put on the horizontal (X) axis and the dependent variable is put on the vertical (Y) axis. _____ _____

4. An appropriate scale is used on each axis depending on the range of data for that axis. _____ _____

5. Appropriate starting points and intervals are used for each axis. _____ _____

6. The whole graph uses the allotted space well. _____ _____

7. Axes are clearly labeled. _____ _____

8. Data are plotted accurately. _____ _____

9. The lines or bars use the space of the graph well. _____ _____

10. The lines or bars accurately represent the trend or lack of it. _____ _____

11. There is a clear title for the graph that names the independent and dependent variables and may state the relationship between them. _____ _____

12. If techniques such as color, texture, or labels are used, an appropriate key is constructed. _____ _____

13. The graph is neat and presentable. _____ _____

14. The graph is easy to interpret. _____ _____

15. The written summary uses appropriate language to concisely and accurately describe the relationship between the independent and dependent variables. _____ _____

Total _____ _____

Authentic Assessment Activities

RUBRIC

Group Work and the Individual

S: The individual's group work skills are very highly developed.

T: The individual shows responsibility by being well prepared for group work and completing all individual tasks on time and with quality. The individual contributes during group discussions and encourages others to contribute. The individual actively listens to others and is tolerant of divergent views. The individual strongly supports his or her own opinions, disagrees agreeably, and works with the group to reach compromises. The individual works with the group to develop and carry out a plan to accomplish the group's goal on time and with quality. The individual promotes positive human relations within the group.

U: The individual's group work skills are generally similar to those of a student receiving a rating of **T,** except that there are some relatively weak aspects to his or her group work.

V: The individual's group work skills are generally similar to those of a student receiving a rating of **W,** except there are some aspects of his or her group work that are better developed.

W: The student is not prepared for group work and does not complete individual tasks on time and/or with quality. The individual contributes too little or excessively dominates group work. The individual does not encourage others to contribute and may inhibit others from contributing. The individual may not support his or her own position or may not be willing to listen to others and reach reasonable compromises. The individual is a poor team player and does not work to develop and carry out a plan to accomplish a task. The individual does not promote positive human relations in the group and may cause negative relations to occur.

X: The individual is a very poor group worker.

CLASSROOM ASSESSMENT LIST

Group Work and the Individual

Element	Assessment Points	
	Possible	**Earned**
1. The individual comes to the group prepared for the group task.	_____	_____
2. The individual completes all individual tasks for the group on time and with quality.	_____	_____
3. The individual participates in a constructive manner.	_____	_____
4. The individual encourages others to participate in a constructive manner.	_____	_____
5. The individual is a good, active listener.	_____	_____
6. The individual supports his/her position in a strong and thoughtful manner.	_____	_____
7. The individual disagrees in an agreeable manner.	_____	_____
8. The individual can reach compromises.	_____	_____
9. The individual shares the responsibility of helping the group get the job done according to directions and on time.	_____	_____
10. The individual promotes positive human relations in the group.	_____	_____
Total	_____	_____

RUBRIC

A Journal

S: The journal is exceptionally insightful and comprehensive. It reveals that the student has thoughtfully and diligently worked at understanding economic and financial concepts.

T: The student has identified personal financial goals with measurable objectives and describes an action plan to achieve them. The section continues with a chronological account of how that action plan was carried out over the duration of the course. Clippings and information from a variety of sources are included. Each section concludes with an evaluation of the degree to which the goals were met and describes plans for improving that element in the future.

U: The journal is like one receiving a rating of **T,** except there are one or two important elements that are not excellent.

V: The journal is like one receiving a rating of **W,** except there are one or two important elements that are well done.

W: Entries are skimpy. It does not appear that the student worked consistently on the journal. The student has not supplied much information. Thoughtful evaluation is missing. The collection of information from newspapers and other sources is missing or very brief. It does not appear that the student committed much time, thought, and action to the journal.

X: The journal is very poorly done.

Note: The journal may contain confidential and personal statements made by the student. It is important that the journal be kept secure by the teacher. The teacher should discuss with the school counselor the school's ground rules for confidentiality and guidelines for what types of information should be brought to the attention of the counselor.

CLASSROOM ASSESSMENT LIST

A Journal

Element	Assessment Points	
	Possible	**Earned**
1. The journal contains regular, chronological entries.	_____	_____
2. Personal financial goals are identified.	_____	_____
3. The journal lists measurable objectives for each goal.	_____	_____
4. An action plan for objectives is included.	_____	_____
5. An organized collection of information related to carrying out the action plan is enclosed.	_____	_____
6. Descriptions of events and feelings are included.	_____	_____
7. Thoughtful reflections including evaluation of the degree to which the personal goals were accomplished are included.	_____	_____
8. The journal includes an organized collection of clippings and other information.	_____	_____
Total	_____	_____

Note: The journal may contain confidential and personal statements made by the student. It is important that the journal be kept secure by the teacher. The teacher should discuss with the school counselor the school's ground rules for confidentiality and guidelines for what types of information should be brought to the attention of the counselor.

RUBRIC

An Issue Controversy

S: The positions are exceptionally well researched. A very thoughtful analysis is done of each position. The final decision is strongly and eloquently supported. Group work is exemplary.

T: The student clearly states the positions in the controversy and makes a thoughtful list of criteria to evaluate each position. The student considers the audience that must be convinced at the end of the controversy. Each position is researched and a thoughtful list of support for the positions has been prepared. Information is properly referenced. The positions are scored on each of the criteria and a position is selected. The decision is thoughtfully and convincingly explained to the target audience. (If two or more people are involved in the consideration of the alternative positions, each thoroughly understands the information for each position and a proper strategy is used to reach a compromise.)

U: The student's work is similar to that receiving a rating of **T,** except that one or two important elements are not excellent.

V: The student's work is similar to that receiving a rating of **W,** except that one or two important elements are well done.

W: The positions are not clearly or completely stated. The list of criteria to evaluate each position is incomplete and/or not fully appropriate. The audience for the final decision has not been thoughtfully considered.
The positions were not explored adequately. The final position is not convincingly supported. If two or more people are involved, appropriate group decision-making strategies of discussion, negotiation, and compromise are not used.

X: The analysis is done very poorly or not at all.

Note: A persuasive oral presentation or a persuasive letter is often the final step in an issue controversy. If so, the rubrics and classroom lists for a writing or an oral presentation could be used. If a group was involved in the process of the issue controversy, each individual should be assigned the persuasive letter to do independently.

CLASSROOM ASSESSMENT LIST
An Issue Controversy

Element	Possible	Earned
Assessment Points		
1. The alternative positions are clearly stated.	_____	_____
2. Criteria for choosing a position are stated. Criteria may be weighted.	_____	_____
3. The audience for the final decision is analyzed and that information is used to make the list of criteria.	_____	_____
4. Research is done for each position.	_____	_____
5. Support is thoughtfully stated for each position.	_____	_____
6. Information from research is properly referenced.	_____	_____
7. Reasons for not supporting each position are thoughtfully stated.	_____	_____
8. If two or more people are involved in the issue controversy, each person in the group understands all reasons for and against each position.	_____	_____
9. Each alternative position is evaluated on each of the criteria.	_____	_____
10. If two or more people are involved in making the decision, appropriate forms of discussion, negotiation, and compromise are used.	_____	_____
11. An alternative is selected and a convincing explanation provided.	_____	_____
Total	_____	_____

Note: A persuasive oral presentation or a persuasive letter is often the final step in an issue controversy. If so, the rubrics and classroom lists for a writing or an oral presentation could be used. If a group was involved in the process of the issue controversy, each individual should be assigned the persuasive letter to do independently.

RUBRIC

A Newspaper Article

S: The article is of exceptional quality. It conveys the story in a smooth and engaging style. The reader's interest is held throughout. Especially appropriate quotes and details are woven into the article. Photographs are highly informative and add much to the story. The headline is memorable.

T: The article is interesting and concise. The theme is immediately apparent, and the article flows smoothly as it is developed. Quotes are used to support the theme without being overused. Appropriate details support the theme. The vocabulary is well chosen to communicate the information to the intended audience. The article is factually correct and ethical. Humor, if used, is in good taste. The headline is appropriate to the story and "grabs" the attention of the reader. Photographs are clear and interesting and show action rather than passive poses. Appropriate captions for photographs are present and in the correct format.

U: The article is like one receiving a rating of **T,** except there are one or two important elements that are not excellent.

V: The article is like one receiving a rating of **W,** except there are one or two important elements that are of good quality.

W: The article reads like the minutes to a meeting. It is not interesting. The theme is unclear and the article is not well organized. Details are missing or not appropriate. Quotes are overused or not used appropriately. Elements of the article may not be in good taste. The headline is not a "grabber." Photographs are of poor quality or are not interesting. Captions for the photographs are incomplete or not in the correct format.

X: The article is of poor quality.

CLASSROOM ASSESSMENT LIST

A Newspaper Article

Element	Assessment Points	
	Possible	**Earned**
1. The facts are correct.	_____	_____
2. Quotes are verbatim.	_____	_____
3. Quotes are used but the whole story is not built on quotes.	_____	_____
4. There is a flow to the writing; it does not read like the minutes to a meeting.	_____	_____
5. The focus of the article is clearly evident in the first paragraph.	_____	_____
6. The readers report having their interest captured immediately.	_____	_____
7. The writing is concise. The limited space is used to the greatest degree.	_____	_____
8. There are enough supporting details for the story.	_____	_____
9. The article is crafted to communicate with the appropriate audience.	_____	_____
10. Humor is used in good taste.	_____	_____
11. The writer has been carefully ethical.	_____	_____
12. The mechanics of language are flawless.	_____	_____
13. The headline is both appropriate to the story and a "grabber."	_____	_____
14. Photographs clearly show what is intended.	_____	_____
15. The photographs are interesting and add information.	_____	_____
16. Captions are accurate and follow the correct format.	_____	_____
Total	_____	_____

RUBRIC

An Oral Presentation

S: The presentation is eloquent. The speaker shows a flair for communicating with the audience. Humor and creativity are clearly present. The speaker is confident and at ease.

T: The presenter speaks in a clear voice that can be heard by all. The speaker shows interest and enthusiasm. The rate of speech is appropriate. The speaker makes eye contact with everyone in the audience. The speaker has no nervous habits that distract the listeners. The speaker is appropriately dressed and has excellent posture. The presentation is organized with a beginning, a body of information, and a conclusion. There is a strong organizing theme to the presentation. There are clear main ideas with transitions between them. The details and examples used make the main ideas meaningful to the audience. Information is complete and accurate. It is clear that the student understands the core curriculum related to this project. Visual aids are used to make the presentation more interesting and meaningful. The visual aids are well done and can be seen by everyone in the audience. The speaker allows time for the audience to think. The speaker involves the audience in some active way in the presentation. The presentation is the appropriate length.

U: The presentation is generally as good as one receiving a rating of **T,** but there are one or two elements of the presentation that are less polished.

V: The presentation is generally similar to one receiving a rating of **W,** but there are one or two elements that are relatively well done.

W: The presenter is difficult to hear. The rate of speaking is too fast or too slow. The speaker does not show much interest and/or enthusiasm in the topic. The speaker may appear to be reading the presentation. Eye contact is made with only some of the audience. The speaker may have nervous habits that distract from the presentation. The speaker is not well groomed. The presentation itself shows little organization. The presentation rambles or it may seem like a list of facts. Details and examples are lacking or not well chosen for the topic and audience. Some information may be incomplete or inaccurate. It is not clear that the student understands the core curriculum related to this project. Visual aids are not well done and cannot be seen by everyone in the audience. The speaker does not involve the audience actively in the presentation. The presentation is not of the appropriate length.

X: The presentation is very poorly done.

CLASSROOM ASSESSMENT LIST
An Oral Presentation

Element	Assessment Points	
	Possible	Earned
1. The speaker can be heard by everyone in the audience.	_____	_____
2. The speaker shows interest and enthusiasm.	_____	_____
3. The rate of speaking is appropriate.	_____	_____
4. The speaker makes eye contact with individuals throughout the audience.	_____	_____
5. The speaker is dressed appropriately, is well groomed, and has excellent posture.	_____	_____
6. The presentation is organized with a beginning, body of information, and conclusion.	_____	_____
7. There is a clear focus to the presentation and the focus is not lost.	_____	_____
8. The main ideas support the focus and there are clear transitions between main ideas.	_____	_____
9. Appropriate support and elaboration are given to the main ideas.	_____	_____
10. It is clear that the speaker knows his/her subject.	_____	_____
11. Visual aids are well done, can be seen by all, and add to the presentation.	_____	_____
12. The speaker allows time for the audience to think.	_____	_____
13. The speaker actively involves his/her audience.	_____	_____
14. The presentation is the appropriate length.	_____	_____
15. The presentation communicates effectively with the intended audience.	_____	_____
16. The presentation is creative and interesting.	_____	_____
Total	_____	_____

RUBRIC

An Original Song with Lyrics

S: The song is outstanding. The music is masterfully composed. The lyrics are memorable. The whole song "works" extremely well for the intended audience.

T: The student has composed the original song using musical form or some other organized structure. Traditional or other symbolic notation is used. The pitch range is appropriate for the voice or instrument used, and the song includes pitches and silences of various durations. A rhythmic pulse can be perceived. Unity and variety are achieved through repetition and contrast and through the use of dynamics and other expressive elements. The lyrics convey the intended message to the target audience. The lyrics and the music work together to achieve the desired effect on the audience.

U: The song is like one receiving a rating of **T,** except there are one or two important elements that are not excellent.

V: The song is like one receiving a rating of **W,** except there are one or two important elements that are well done.

W: The song is not very original. The student does not make use of an organized structure or appropriate notation. The pitch range is not well matched to the voice or instrument used. Pitches and silences are not planned well. A rhythmic pulse is absent or inappropriate. There is too little variety or too much contrast in the song. The words do not convey the content of the message well and the music and lyrics do not work well together.

X: The song is very poorly done or completely unoriginal.

CLASSROOM ASSESSMENT LIST
An Original Song with Lyrics

Element	Assessment Points	
	Possible	Earned
1. The song is original.	_____	_____
2. The pitch range is appropriate for the instrument or voice.	_____	_____
3. Traditional or symbolic notation is correctly used.	_____	_____
4. A rhythmic pulse can be perceived.	_____	_____
5. It is written in musical form, or in some other organized structure.	_____	_____
6. Unity and variety are achieved through repetition and contrast.	_____	_____
7. It makes use of dynamics and other expressive elements.	_____	_____
8. It makes use of pitches and silences of various durations.	_____	_____
9. The lyrics convey the intended message to the target audience.	_____	_____
10. The music and lyrics work together.	_____	_____
Total	_____	_____

RUBRIC

A Poster

S: The poster is outstanding, creative, and communicates information to the audience in an eloquent manner.

T: The theme of the poster is clear when you first look at it. As you study it, more and more information comes out. There are main ideas (the general) supported by appropriate details (the specific). There is a "wholeness" about the poster and it is not just a collection of pieces. Main ideas are connected to a theme. Information is complete and accurate. The concepts and information used show that the student clearly understands the core curriculum related to this project. Space, shapes, textures, and colors are used to provide information and to make the poster easier for the viewer to understand. Pictures, photographs, drawings, diagrams, graphs, and other devices add clarity and information. The words used are appropriate for the topic and audience. The form of the poster is appropriate for the author's intended purpose. The work is very neat and presentable.

U: The poster is as good as a poster receiving a rating of **T,** but there are one or two important elements that are not as well developed.

V: The poster is similar to a poster receiving a rating of **W,** but there are some important elements that are more well developed.

W: The poster is difficult to understand even when its purpose is explained by the author. The poster seems like a collection of pieces without clear main ideas hooking them together. Some information may be incomplete or inaccurate. The student does not demonstrate a mastery of the core curriculum related to this project. Space, shapes, textures, and colors are not used or used in an appropriate manner to add information to the poster or make it easier for the audience to understand. Pictures, photographs, drawings, diagrams, graphs, and other devices are not used or used inappropriately. The words used are not clear. The form of the poster may not be the best one for the author's intended purpose. The work is not neat and presentable.

X: The poster is very poorly done.

CLASSROOM ASSESSMENT LIST
A Poster

Element	Assessment Points	
	Possible	**Earned**

1. The main theme is clear when you first look at it. _____ _____

2. Appropriate and accurate main ideas support the theme. _____ _____

3. There is a wholeness about the poster. It does not seem like a collection of information. _____ _____

4. The information in the poster is accurate and shows that the student thoroughly understands the concepts. _____ _____

5. Space, shapes, textures, and colors provide information themselves and add to the overall effectiveness of the poster. _____ _____

6. Pictures, photographs, drawings, diagrams, graphs, or other similar devices add to the overall effectiveness of the poster. _____ _____

7. The format of the poster is appropriate to the task and to the audience for which it is intended. _____ _____

8. The poster is very neat and presentable. _____ _____

9. The poster is creative and interesting. _____ _____

Total _____ _____

RUBRIC

A Research Report

S: This research report is eloquent and exceptionally thoughtful and informative. It achieves its purpose with the intended audience in a most masterful manner.

T: The thesis statement clearly defines the topic and describes what the author intends to say or prove. The introduction explains the purpose of the paper, provides the context for and the significance of the topic, and lays out the style and organizational pattern to be used in the paper. The audience is engaged immediately. Paragraphs are logically ordered with effective transitions between them. Each paragraph has a clear topic sentence and appropriate supporting details. The ideas and details all work together in a smooth manner to develop the thesis. The conclusion effectively demonstrates that the author has proved what was set out to be proved in the thesis statement. The paper is concise and uses appropriate vocabulary for the topic and audience. Appropriate and quality information sources are used. It is very clear that the author has mastered the concepts involved. It is also very clear that the author's own thinking is paramount throughout the paper. When other people's ideas are used, the author gives proper credit. If used, graphics add to the clarity of the paper and help it achieve its purpose. All format elements including footnotes, headings and subheadings, spacing and margins, and the bibliography are correct. The conventions of standard written English are correct. The paper is very neat and presentable.

U: This paper is generally as good as that receiving a rating of **T,** but it is uneven with some relatively less-developed areas.

V: This paper is generally similar to that receiving a rating of **W,** but it has one or two areas that are relatively better developed.

W: The thesis statement is unclear as to the focus of the topic and/or what the author intends to prove regarding it. The introduction does not effectively explain the purpose of the paper and/or provide the context for the thesis and/or lay out the pattern of organization that the paper will follow. The body of the paper contains ideas that support the thesis, but their organization is not effective. Some paragraphs do not have clear main ideas and/or do not contain appropriate supporting details. The ideas seem like a list of points without effective transitions. The conclusion does not convince the reader that the author has proved what was intended to be proved and it is not clear that the author has mastered the concepts involved. The paper is wordy or underdeveloped. Information sources used are not of high quality. The paper seems like a summary of other people's thinking and the thinking of the author is not evident throughout. Graphics detract from the report or do not help it achieve its purpose. Format elements including footnotes, headings and subheadings, spacing and margins, and the bibliography are not all correct. The conventions of standard written English are not all correct. The paper is not neat or presentable.

X: The paper is extremely weak in most or all areas.

CLASSROOM ASSESSMENT LIST

A Research Report

Element	Assessment Points	
	Possible	**Earned**
1. The thesis statement is clearly stated.	_____	_____
2. The introduction explains the purpose of the paper, provides context for the report, and gives an overview of the report.	_____	_____
3. The body of the paper is organized into paragraphs with clear main ideas and appropriate supporting details.	_____	_____
4. The conclusion effectively demonstrates that the author has accomplished his or her purpose.	_____	_____
5. It is clear that the author knows the core content of this topic.	_____	_____
6. It is clear that the author's own thinking is the focus of this report.	_____	_____
7. It is clear that the author has used quality informational sources and referenced them correctly.	_____	_____
8. Graphics, if used, add to the clarity of information in the report.	_____	_____
9. All format elements are correct.	_____	_____
10. The mechanics of English are correct.	_____	_____
11. The report is neat and presentable.	_____	_____
Total	_____	_____

Authentic Assessment Activities

RUBRIC

A Self-Assessment

S: The student shows exceptional insight and clarity into the quality of his or her own learning.

T: The student views himself or herself as a learner working to understand economic concepts. The self-assessment is more than a description of the external products of learning. It focuses on the internal processes of the learner. The learner describes how concepts and information are used, how the thinking skills of learning are used, and how his or her attitudes and mental habits influence the learning. The learner discusses how he or she has used classroom lists and models of excellent work to guide his or her work. The learner has an awareness of his or her own learning style and discusses preferences for product format and audience. The student also identifies how individual and group work influence his or her learning. The student is honest and perceptive in identifying and describing his or her strengths and weaknesses and states ways to improve.

U: The student's work is similar to that receiving a rating of **T,** but there are areas of lesser quality. The self-assessment is not evenly of high quality.

V: The student's work is generally at the level of a **W** rating, but there are elements that are thoughtful and show some insight.

W: Overall, the student's self-assessment shows little in-depth thinking and insight. The student tends to focus on describing the products of learning rather than how he or she is progressing as a learner. The learner has little to say about how he or she used the classroom lists and models of excellent work.

X: The self-assessment is incomplete and poorly done.

CLASSROOM ASSESSMENT LIST

A Self-Assessment

Element	Assessment Points	
	Possible	Earned

1. The student describes how he or she has used classroom assessment lists and models of excellent student work to guide and assess his/her own work.

2. The student describes how he or she has learned to use concepts and information.

3. The student describes how he or she has learned to use thinking skills.

4. The student describes how his or her attitudes and habits of mind have influenced his or her learning.

5. The student describes how individual and group work contribute to his or her learning.

6. The student describes the actions that he or she will take to improve as a learner.

Total

Authentic Assessment Activities

RUBRIC
A Skit

S: The skit is exceptional. The story line and characters use creativity and/or humor to send a clear message to the intended audience. All the elements of acting are very well done.

T: The skit does an excellent job of communicating the intended message to the intended audience. Everyone can be heard and seen. The information and dialogue are appropriate to the topic and audience. The characters are well suited to the topic and audience and they are well developed by the actors and/or actresses. The props add to the effectiveness of the skit. The skit is organized and focused on the topic and is of an appropriate length.

U: The skit is like those receiving a rating of **T,** except there are some important elements that are not excellent. This skit is unevenly excellent.

V: The skit is like those receiving a rating of **W,** except there are some important elements that are good.

W: The skit does a poor job of communicating the intended message to the intended audience. Some of the characters cannot be heard and/or seen well. The characters may not be well suited to the topic and/or audience. The characters may not be developed well by the actors and/or actresses. The props are lacking, do not add much, or are even distracting. The skit is not organized or focused and is too long or too short. Verbal and/or non-verbal information in the skit is not accurate.

X: The skit is very poor.

CLASSROOM ASSESSMENT LIST

A Skit

Element	Assessment Points	
	Possible	Earned
1. The speakers can be heard by everyone in the audience.	_____	_____
2. The dialogue is appropriate to both the topic and audience.	_____	_____
3. The characters are well suited to the topic of the skit.	_____	_____
4. The characters are developed by the actors and actresses.	_____	_____
5. The props used in the skit add to the interest and message of the skit.	_____	_____
6. Everyone can see the actions in the skit.	_____	_____
7. The skit is organized and focused on the topic.	_____	_____
8. The information, both spoken and non-verbal, in the skit is accurate and appropriate to the topic.	_____	_____
9. The skit is the appropriate length.	_____	_____
Total	_____	_____

RUBRIC

A Slideshow or Photo Essay

S: The slide show or photo essay is an outstanding presentation of the theme. The technical quality of the pictures is excellent. The audience is powerfully affected by the set of pictures.

T: The student has taken pictures that are well focused and lighted. Each picture is composed to clearly show what is intended. The entire set of photographs is organized, sequenced smoothly, and contains a clear theme. The set has its intended effect on the audience. It is clear that the student understands the core concepts of the theme and has chosen pictures well. Titles and other statements add information to the display. For the photo essay, the pictures are mounted and displayed in an attractive and very presentable manner.

U: The set of pictures is similar to that receiving a rating of **T,** except there are important elements that are not all excellent.

V: The set of pictures is similar to that receiving a rating of **W,** except there are some elements that are of good quality.

W: The student has taken pictures that are not well focused or lighted. The pictures are not well composed. They do not clearly show what is intended. The entire set of pictures is not well organized and it is uneven in its presentation of the theme. It is not clear that the student understands the core concepts. The pictures are not well chosen to present the theme to the target audience. The set does not have its intended effect on that audience. Titles and other statements are missing, incomplete, or inaccurate. For the photo essay, the pictures are not mounted and displayed in a presentable manner.

X: The slide show or photo essay is very poorly done.

Note: If an oral presentation (live or taped) accompanies the show, it can be assessed by using the rubric and classroom list for an oral presentation. If a written script accompanies the set, it can be assessed by using the rubric and classroom list for a writing.

CLASSROOM ASSESSMENT LIST

A Slideshow or Photo Essay

Element	Assessment Points	
	Possible	**Earned**
1. Each picture in the set is well composed to clearly show what is intended.	_____	_____
2. Each picture is well focused and lighted appropriately.	_____	_____
3. The sequence of pictures has a clear theme.	_____	_____
4. The sequence is organized.	_____	_____
5. There is a smooth flow of pictures through the set.	_____	_____
6. The sequence has its intended effect on the audience.	_____	_____
7. It is clear that the author understands the core concepts related to this topic and has chosen pictures appropriately.	_____	_____
8. Titles and other statements contribute to the theme and purpose of the set of pictures.	_____	_____
9. For the photo essay, the pictures are mounted and displayed in an attractive and presentable manner.	_____	_____
Total	_____	_____

Note: If an oral presentation (live or taped) accompanies the show, it can be assessed by using the rubric and classroom list for an oral presentation. If a written script accompanies the show, it can be assessed by using the rubric and classroom list for a writing.

RUBRIC

A Survey

S: The student's work is superb. The survey questions are exceptional in all elements. Great care is taken to collect appropriate, valid, and reliable data. The survey is conducted in an extremely professional manner. The record keeping is flawless. The summary is an exceptional analysis of the survey findings.

T: The student clearly defines the purpose of the survey. The student identifies the population to be surveyed. The student has a strategy to collect the data from a representative sampling of the population being surveyed. The questions are focused, clearly worded, and grammatically correct. The questions are written in a manner that draws unbiased responses. The questions are formatted in a way that will make responses to the survey easy. The student conducts the survey in a polite and professional manner. The student clearly states the purpose of the survey to the people being surveyed. The student carefully records the responses during the interview process. The summary clearly communicates the overall findings of the survey.

U: The work is generally like that receiving a rating of **T,** except there are some elements that are not excellent.

V: The work is generally like that receiving a rating of **W,** except there are some elements that are well done.

W: The purpose of the survey is not clearly defined. The population to be surveyed is not identified. The student does not have a plan to collect valid and reliable data. The survey is not taken from a representative sampling of the population being surveyed. The questions are not focused, clearly worded, or grammatically correct. The questions are written in a way that biases the responses. The questions are not formatted so that responding to the survey will be easy. The student conducts the survey in an impolite and unprofessional manner. The purpose of the survey is not clearly stated to the people being surveyed. The responses are not recorded during the interview process. The overall findings are not clearly communicated.

X: The work is very poorly prepared and executed in all areas.

Note: The written summary of the findings can be assessed using the rubric and classroom list for a writing.

CLASSROOM ASSESSMENT LIST

A Survey

Element	Assessment Points	
	Possible	**Earned**
1. The purpose of the survey is clearly defined.	_____	_____
2. The population to be surveyed is identified.	_____	_____
3. A clear strategy for collecting the data from a representative sampling of the population is developed.	_____	_____
4. The questions are focused, clearly worded, and grammatically correct.	_____	_____
5. The questions draw unbiased responses from those being surveyed.	_____	_____
6. It is easy to respond to the survey questions.	_____	_____
7. The survey is conducted in a polite and professional manner.	_____	_____
8. The purpose of the survey is clearly stated to the people being surveyed.	_____	_____
10. The responses to the survey are carefully recorded during the interview process.	_____	_____
11. The summary clearly communicates the findings of the survey.	_____	_____

Note: The written summary of the findings can be assessed using the rubric and classroom list for a writing.

RUBRIC

A Writing

S: The student's work is unusually thoughtful, complete, and clear. It shows a very high level of conceptual understanding and ability to communicate with a specified audience.

T: The student's work is excellent. The student clearly understands the task and brings appropriate concepts to bear. Relevant and appropriate information supports the concepts. Appropriate vocabulary is used. The writing is very well organized and focused throughout. It clearly shows that the student has used higher-order thinking. The purpose of the writing is successfully carried out. The writing communicates well with its intended audience. Where necessary, references are properly made. Spelling and other language mechanics are excellent. The work is very neat and presentable. (If needed, visuals such as drawings, diagrams, graphic organizers, tables, charts, or graphs are well used to support the writing.)

U: The student's work is generally excellent. Some important elements are less than excellent. The work is uneven.

V: The student's work is generally poor. However, some important elements are rather well done, so the work is not entirely poor.

W: The student's work is poor. The student does not understand the task clearly. Some concepts are inappropriately used. Some concepts central to the topic are not used. Inappropriate or inadequate information is used to support the concepts. Vocabulary is not well selected. The work is not well organized or focused and higher-order thinking is not evident. The writing does not successfully carry out its purpose. The writing does not communicate well with the intended audience. The work has errors in language mechanics that make the work more difficult to understand. References, if needed, are missing or incorrectly made. The work is not neat and presentable. (If needed, visuals such as drawings, diagrams, graphic organizers, tables, charts, or graphs are missing or not well used.)

X: The work is very poor.

CLASSROOM ASSESSMENT LIST

A Writing

Element	Assessment Points	
	Possible	**Earned**
1. The student uses appropriate concepts correctly.	_____	_____
2. The student uses appropriate information to support the concepts used.	_____	_____
3. Appropriate vocabulary is used.	_____	_____
4. The writing is organized and focused.	_____	_____
5. Higher-order thinking is evident.	_____	_____
6. The purpose of the writing is clearly carried out.	_____	_____
7. References, if needed, are properly made.	_____	_____
8. Language mechanics are correct.	_____	_____
9. The writing is neat and presentable.	_____	_____
10. If needed, visuals such as drawings, diagrams, graphic organizers, tables, charts, or graphs are well used to support the writing.	_____	_____
Total	_____	_____